The Parent Handbook

A quick reference guide to positive communication during difficult moments

By Leslie Farwell Leline

Copyright 2008 By Leslie Farwell Leline

All rights reserved.

No part of this book may be reproduced or transmitted in any form or by any means, electronic or mechanical, including photocopy, recording or information and retrieval system without permission from the author.

ISBN: 1-4392-0918-9
ISBN-13: 9781439209189

Printed By:
Book Surge
Charleston, SC

To order more copies,
email Leslie F. Leline
leslie@theparenthandbook.org

For Caitlin and Erin
I love you up to the sky

Many thanks to Paul, Robin, Joan, Kate, Bob, Carol, Charlie, Barnaby, Erin, Cait and Andy for your time, inspiration and wisdom.

Author's Note:

I am a mother and a teacher. I have been raising children and teaching preschool for the past 25 years, and during that time I have seen certain behavior issues arise again and again. After many years of helping parents* address these issues, I have some insights I'd like to share.

Parenting is not an easy job. It is a job that requires consistency and selflessness every single day. Successful parenting, I believe, requires a balance of love, communication and guidance. This book, I hope, will bring some clarity and direction to the job.

If you find something in this book that works for you, that is great. I am delighted.

If you disagree with anything I offer in this book, please, don't use it. I respect your decision and admire you for thinking it through.

My hope in sharing my ideas is to make a difference in one child's life, to open one person's mind to a new approach, or to help one parent take a breath before reacting.

I wish you well and remind you to be proud of every effort you make to do your best as a parent.

Sincerely, Leslie

*please note that I use the word 'parent' loosely to include all caregivers regardless of gender, marital status, or living arrangements.

Table of Contents:

Introduction – Notes from the Author	xiii
All Ages	
Chapter 1 – Forgive Yourself and Try Again	1
Chapter 2 – Consistency between Parents	3
Chapter 3 – Keeping Your Cool	5
Chapter 4 – Please Stop Yelling	9
Chapter 5 – Do I Have to Say It Again?	13
Chapter 6 – TV, Computers, Movies	17
Chapter 7 – Other Kids' Behavior	19
Chapter 8 – Bribes and Threats	21
Chapter 9 – Should I Ignore It?	23
Chapter 10 – Discipline in Public?	25
1-3 years old	
Chapter 11 – Spoiling My Baby	29
Chapter 12 – Such a Temper for a Toddler	
– 3 variations	31
Chapter 13 – She's in My Stuff!	37
Chapter 14 – Jealous of the Baby – 5 variations	39
Chapter 15 – Screaming Tot	47
Chapter 16 – But 'He' Doesn't Have To!	
– 2 variations	49

4-6 years old

Chapter 17 – Pretend Play – 2 variations ... 53
Chapter 18 – Talking Back – 2 variations ... 55
Chapter 19 – Discipline is Not Working - 5 variations ... 59
Chapter 20 – Scared at Night ... 69
Chapter 21 – Restaurant Behavior ... 71
Chapter 22 – Tears and Anger ... 75
Chapter 23 – Death of a Grandparent ... 79
Chapter 24 – Interrupting ... 81
Chapter 25 – Bullying at Four ... 83
Chapter 26 – Baby Talk ... 85
Chapter 27 – Son Won't Leave ... 87
Chapter 28 – Toy Guns ... 89
Chapter 29 – Lies About My Child ... 91
Chapter 30 – Fear of a Crowd ... 95
Chapter 31 – Time Out ... 97
Chapter 32 – Reacts by Hitting ... 99
Chapter 33 – Picky Eaters – 5 variations ... 103

7-10 years old

Chapter 34 – Picking Up Toys ... 111
Chapter 35 – No Hitting, Ever ... 113
Chapter 36 – Aggressive Behavior ... 117
Chapter 37 – Sassy Mouth ... 119
Chapter 38 – Other Parent Blames My Child ... 121
Chapter 39 – Teacher Picks on My Son ... 123
Chapter 40 – Playground Crisis ... 129
Chapter 41 – 5th Grader Doesn't Care ... 131
Chapter 42 – Bright but Pushing Obnoxious ... 133
Chapter 43 – How Much Truth to Tell About Sex ... 137

11-17 years old

Chapter 44 – Different Parenting Styles	141
Chapter 45 – Friendship Trouble	143
Chapter 46 – Quick to Give Up	147
Chapter 47 – Daughter Wants To Quit Band	149
Chapter 48 – Apathetic Teen	153
Chapter 49 – Sleeping Late	155
Chapter 50 – Her Friend is SO Mean	157
Chapter 51 – Curfew	161
Chapter 52 – Dad's Difficulty with Dating Daughter	165
Chapter 53 – Parent Attacks My Parenting	167
Chapter 54 – Letting Teens Drink	171
Conclusion – Parting Thoughts	173

Introduction

The words you choose to speak to your children cause them to form an opinion of who they are. Choose wisely.

Choose words that build self-esteem, respect and trust. Those words, together with unconditional love and positive guidance, create the fundamentals for successful parenting.

Every chapter in this book leads you through a difficult situation keeping these fundamentals in mind.

As parents, our goal is to instill in our children the best morals and values we can at a young age. Beyond that, we must teach them the skills they need to be able to cope and conduct themselves successfully while keeping their values intact. All this while building and preserving our children's self-esteem.

My goal is that as you read this book you feel proud of the time and effort you are putting into your parenting skills and that you can delight in the incredible results as you see your children grow into reliable, considerate young adults.

On behalf of your child,

Thank you for choosing to read on.

Thank you for making an effort to do the best job you can as a parent.

Chapter 1: Forgive Yourself and Try Again

Q: *Are there people who are perfect parents and have all the answers?*

A: Not on this planet!
This is a HARD JOB.

There is no schooling required before you give birth, so you have to learn on the job. Your most readily available resource is the memory of what your parents did when raising you. Sometimes that is not the way you want to raise your children.

You have to take a deep breath, think bigger and find a new answer. Ask questions, read, listen and keep trying. When you realize that you handled something poorly, be honest with your children. Tell them that you can see that you could have handled it differently and that you will try to think about different options next time. Let your children know that you are doing the best you can and you are trying to learn all the time to do even better.

In doing that, you will be setting an excellent example for forgiving yourself, being honest and constantly trying to improve – what a great role model for your child!

Chapter 2:
Consistency between Parents

Q: *What happens when my partner and I have different ideas about how to parent?*

A: Whatever your differences are, talk them through and find a compromise to get you both on the same page before you talk to your child. Consistency between parents is very important for the solid foundation of a child. By working together, you will help your child to build trust in his parents and to understand that you respect him and each other.

It is a real problem if you parent differently. It ultimately causes trouble in your relationship and in your individual relationships with your child. When you each treat your child differently, it causes tremendous confusion for him as well as doubt, mistrust, and frustration. This will lead to manipulation and defiance. It is a lose-lose situation for parents of the same child to be using different parenting rules and techniques.

Is it ok with both of you for your child to eat sweets right before dinner? To watch four hours of TV? To speak rudely to you? To be on the phone at midnight?

From the smallest of details, as caretakers you have to be on the same wavelength with the same goals and limits. As you and your partner learn to parent similarly, your child will feel more secure, develop more self-discipline, and have more respect for your decisions as parents.

Chapter 3: Keeping Your Cool

Q: *When everything is so upsetting and chaotic in a moment of bad behavior and anger, it seems unrealistic to be able to stay calm and figure out the right words to use and the proper consequences! How do you keep your cool?*

A: Walk away.

Be honest and say, "I am so angry that I can't talk to you right now." It is ok to delay a consequence temporarily while you regain composure. It only takes a minute for that intense emotion of anger to dissipate, and then you can walk back in and talk to your child rationally, with respect and compassion.

Even at a young age, children can understand if you tell them you need a minute to think about how to handle this situation. You can ask them to sit in one place while you take a minute to calm down and that you will then be ready to talk about what happened. Or with very young or out-of-control children, if you can't walk away, you can simply hold them tight on your lap but say nothing until you have taken deep breaths. In fact, if they are out of control, hold them until *their* moment of anger passes also before you begin talking. Holding them tightly provides them with a safe yet controlled place to be while they are emotionally and perhaps physically charged.

As children get older, it is a good idea to involve them in the decision-making. Once you have regained your calm, you might say, "I have thought about what you did, this is why it was inappropriate…, what do you think the consequence should be?" The more we get children involved in thinking through the cause and effect of their actions, the more we are helping them learn to discipline themselves. That is our ultimate goal.

If there is a situational reason you can't walk away during the moment of anger, such as a spilled gallon of milk on the floor, then, without exploding, say, "I need to take care of this but I am too angry to talk to you right now. Go to the other room. When I calm down I will come and talk to you" or "Please help me clean up but I do not want to talk right now. I am upset that this happened. We will talk later when I am calm."

It might seem hard to not explode, but with practice and conscious effort, it is indeed possible. In the meantime, if you do loose your cool, just catch yourself and stop as soon as possible. Say to your child, "I am sorry I blew up at you. I am learning that angry behavior does not accomplish anything and I will try to stop yelling. Now I have calmed down and I need to talk about what just happened."

Our children need to know that you make mistakes and then you try again. That's what you want them to learn. It is important for them to understand that they are good people and that they should keep trying. If you present yourselves as infallible, if you make them feel as if they are the only ones to make a mistake, it sets an impossible standard for them to live up to. So show them your imperfect self, and let them know that you are still learning and doing the best you can. And keep striving to wait until the height of emotion passes before you talk.

Chapter 4:
Please Stop Yelling

Q: *Is it ever ok to yell?*

A: Only if your child is about to do something that will endanger his or someone else's life. If he is about to walk out into traffic, yell. If he has just grabbed a sharp knife and is running, yell. If he is backing the car out of the garage and there is a bike behind the car, yell.

Other than in life-threatening situations, it is inappropriate to yell. Yelling is demeaning. Yelling makes you sound as if you are saying, "You are a disappointment and a failure." That is NOT the message you want to send. Everyone makes bad choices sometimes. Imagine yelling at a three-year-old who broke a plate. Is this going to change the fact that the plate is broken? Will it make him feel scared and intimidated? Now imagine yelling at your teenager because he got a bad grade. Is that going to motivate him to do better? Will it let him know that you have a bad temper and you do not treat him with respect?

The most important goal as a parent is to raise your child with self-esteem. Everything else can be learned, but your child needs to have self-respect and self-love to survive. This makes it possible for him to have the courage and desire to learn. Yelling diminishes that esteem. What you can do instead of yelling, is speak with clarity and respect to help your child learn from the inappropriate choices he makes so that he will build the skills and knowledge to make better choices next time.

No matter how old your child is, or how much yelling has gone on in the past, you can tell him that today you have decided that it is not ok to yell and you are going to try your best to stop that. In the heat of the moment, you can take a deep breath, go to your room to cool down, or go for a jog. When you come back you will be calm and can use a respectful voice when you talk about what upset you.

Bad behavior from your child does not call for rude behavior from you. Your child listens to everything you say. The words you use, the tone and the volume of your voice, all have a tremendous and lasting impact on your child. Be a role model and show your child that communicating with a calm, compassionate voice gets more accomplished than yelling.

As soon as the yelling begins, all ears go deaf. No one listens during a time of heightened emotion. So just walk away until you can let go of the heightened anger. Then talk with your child about what happened and what to do about it. With a young child, you are a dictator. You decide the consequence. With an older child, involve him in the problem-solving and work together to find a solution.

Through calm discussion of logical consequences, you will build trust with your child and a respect for each other as individuals. Then you will have used the opportunity to teach great life skills instead of teaching him to turn a deaf ear.

Chapter 5:
Do I Have To Say It Again?

Q: *Sometimes I feel like a broken record and I just don't see the point in repeating myself again. Shouldn't my kids get it after hearing it ten times?*

A: The reality is you have to keep repeating yourself for at least seventeen years!

The more dangerous the potential behavior, the more times you will need to repeat yourself. Some things you have to repeat ten times, some things you have to repeat two thousand times.

Let's start with things that are dangerous. Just as we tell our toddlers over and over not to touch the hot stove, we will tell our teens not to drink and drive. It may get tiring, but it is part of our job.

When your child is in high school going to a party, you will repeat, "Ok, we need to review – there is no drinking and driving, and if the driver has a drink, call me and I'll come get you at any time of night." Your child may say, "I am fifteen and you have been telling me this for years," and you reply, "I know. My job is to keep you safe, and to do that I need to keep repeating this. So, there is no drinking and driving …"

Keep saying it!

You have to help your child feel strong about the choices she makes and to believe in herself so she will have the strength to make those choices. All of your hard work and endless repetition is helping her build self-esteem and self-discipline so she can get through the scary, dangerous stuff and have fun.

On another note, if you find yourself repeating requests for mundane chores, Stop! You are being ineffective. Instead of repeating yourself, there should be a consequence. If you have asked your child to pick up her clothes and put them in her room instead of in a pile on the living room floor, and she has not responded, repeating yourself ten times will have no effect. She will instead learn that when you ask her to do something, she doesn't really have to do it because there is no consequence, you just keep nagging.

Rather, if you have already asked her once, you may offer one reminder. Then, walk over to her, and ask her to stop whatever she is doing. "Please go turn off the TV" (unplug the iPod, put down the book, hang up the phone). You need to pick up your clothes right now. When that is done, you can resume your activity." If she cries or fusses, stay calm, and simply remind her that she may continue her activity as soon as the clothes are picked up.

Have a discussion with your child and let her know that while she is living in your house, she will help with chores just like everyone else. "We all make messes and we all help clean up. If I ask you to do something reasonable, and you do not respond, I will end all activity for you until you choose to cooperate and behave as a functioning part of the household." (Be sure your requests for help are age appropriate)

The next time you ask her to do something and she responds, be sure to thank her for her help in keeping the house a home.

Chapter 6:
TV, Computers & Movies

Q: *My son seems to be acting out more as he spends more time in front of his computer games. Do you think there is a correlation?*

A: Absolutely.

Visual stimulation has a huge impact on a child. It is confusing and almost impossible for a child to watch or play games that involve hurting, killing, rude voices, inappropriate behavior, stealing, or bombing, and then not imitate any of that behavior. The more violence he watches the more acceptable it becomes in his mind. It becomes "normal" to him and does not seem out of line.

As parents, you have control for many years over what your child watches or sees on a screen. There are millions of games and shows that demonstrate good values, that are about cooperation, learning, teamwork, investigation, compassion, patience, problem- solving, nature, creative thinking – expose your child to these! There is an endless supply of great computer games and videos that have a positive and/or educational message. Put your child's hours in front of a screen to good work! Use them to educate and reinforce your family values and beliefs.

Try to limit the number of hours spent at the computer and TV by encouraging other interests. If your child loves carpentry work, buy tools and build a real door together. If he thinks that making tie-dyed t-shirts is the coolest thing in the world, you can create those together for Christmas gifts. Collect and identify bugs and try painting some of your favorites. Get a junked motor, take it apart in the garage and see if you can both work to put it back together.

These activities take more effort than flipping on the screen, but if you respond enthusiastically to your child's interests you will build his confidence and at the same time strengthen your relationship with him

Parenting is our job. Make the extra effort and take the time to be an effective, creative parent. A screen is a poor replacement for human interaction.

Chapter 7:
Other Kids' Behavior

Q: *How do you deal with parents whose rules for their children are so different from your own?*

A: If adults are in your home with their children and a child is behaving in a way that you consider inappropriate, be very frank and explain that the behavior is not allowed at your house. Tell them that you respect the fact that the behavior may be considered ok at their house, but the rules at your house apply to all children in the house – family and friends alike.

Unfortunately, you may realize that some good friends have such very different parenting techniques that you choose to spend limited time with them. You may not be willing to subject your child to what you see as inappropriate role modeling. In this case, invite their children to your house where you can keep an eye on things rather than having your child go to their house where you feel uncomfortable with the family's rules.

Sometimes sticky situations come up with family members, and you just have to be polite yet blunt. "Sis, I love you, but I'd like you to know that it is important to me that we not talk about food in relation to it making us fat. I want my children to think of food as something we eat to stay alive, not as a self-image issue, so I am asking you not to talk at my house about food in connection with body image. Thank you."

Usually if you present your rules calmly and with grace, other parents accept them even if they disagree.

Chapter 8:
Bribes and Threats

Q: *What do you think about using bribes and threats for discipline techniques?*

A: In general, they are bad ideas.

Discipline is the hardest part of parenting. For that reason, it is also the most neglected part of the job. It is easier to ignore a child's unacceptable behavior or to tell your partner to deal with it than to carefully think through an effective discipline technique and use it consistently.

Ideally, we shouldn't use rewards or threats. That is not to say it is never going to happen. But as a rule, bribes teach children to push the limits to see what the payoff is going to be, and threats teach children to ignore us because there are no consequences to those empty threats.

Often, bribes and threats are used in a hurry without much thought. They are a quick "remedy" for the moment but often have negative long-term effects. They are techniques that are used because we have not thought through a logical, calm way to help our child understand what the acceptable behavior is in the situation. We have not taken the time to problem-solve with our child so that he can learn from his mistake.

Remember, a difficult situation is the perfect time to teach your child self-discipline, problem solving and respect. What an opportunity you are giving up if you dish out a bribe or threat instead of using the opportunity to teach.

Chapter 9:
Should I Ignore It?

Q: *Should I ignore bad behavior?*

A: NO.

If you ignore a behavior you are telling your child that that behavior is acceptable.

Note: The exception of course is if you have previously told your child that you will be intentionally ignoring him and not responding to some behavior that he is using to get your attention, such as whining or yelling. You will choose to ignore him until he finds an appropriate way to converse with you. In this situation, you could say, "I will not respond to that voice, please come back when you have found a polite way to speak to me," and then you do indeed ignore him if he continues whining.

Chapter 10:
Discipline in Public

Q: *When my child is being naughty out in public, I yell and swear at her and other parents give me a dirty look, but what else am I supposed to do?*

A: First, yelling and swearing are not only rude but they are also demeaning. Being spoken to like that destroys self-esteem and eats away at the very trust and respect you would like to have from your child.

Some people think that adults need not show children respect. Or that because they are the grown-ups, they can speak to their child rudely. In this case, if your child yells or swears at you, you have no grounds to be upset - she is doing what you have taught her.

Second, take her hand and tell your friends that you'll be right back. Do not make a public display out of your discipline. Go to a private place to talk. Respect the fact that it would be very embarrassing for anyone to be scolded in public and if you want to build a relationship of trust, you must show respect to her. Go outside or to the bathroom or the car. Have a chat about what went wrong and decide then if you can go back inside and enjoy yourselves, or if you need to go home and try again another day.

One to three years old

Look into those eyes
Deep inside
Behind the temper
Behind the attitude
There he truly is
Waiting
Patiently
For someone to look
To really look
To see in those eyes
And realize
The magnificence
Of the child

Chapter 11: Spoiling Babies

Q: *My mom says I feed my baby too often. She thinks my child is spoiled and manipulating me. My baby is four months old and cries a lot. So I rock her, hold her, bathe her and feed her. I don't let her cry very long. She is so tiny; I can't believe her crying is manipulative. Am I wrong?*

A: No, you are exactly right. You cannot spoil a baby. At four months all they need is warmth, safety, love and food, so give it all freely. Be there for her and all her baby needs.

There are plenty of years ahead when you will have to decide when to say 'yes' and 'no' to a child. Right now just enjoy the simplicity of fulfilling her every need. Hold her, comfort her, feed her and let her know you are there to keep her safe in the world.

Tell your mom you will work out the dynamics of her social behavior when she is up and walking!

Chapter 12:
Such a Temper for a Toddler

Q: *I don't know what to do with my toddler. Her doctor says she is healthy and normal, but she is fifteen months old and today she tipped the dog water over seven times. She just doesn't care when I get mad or yell. I'll be honest; today I hit her because I couldn't take it anymore. She won't sit still. I can't read to her and she throws things instead of talking to me. At fifteen months, my older daughter would sit for an hour or more and listen to stories and was already helping me put toys away!*

A: It is possible that your elder daughter is an auditory learner (hearing) and the younger is a kinesthetic learner (touching). She tips the dog water over because that is how you learn what happens when you tip it. She tipped it over seven times because you never took it away or put her in a different room. At her age, a child's job is to investigate and explore. Allow her to do exactly that and set up her environment so that she will not get into things that upset you.

Q: *But she doesn't understand when I tell her to stop tipping it over.*

A: She is so young. If she were four, you could expect her to understand and behave on a more cognitive level. She doesn't understand because the bowl remains there with water in it for her to tip. A child of fifteen months needs you as the parent to modify her environment because at that age she learns through hands-on exploration. Perhaps you could put the dog water behind a door gate where the dog can get to it and she cannot. At times, rearranging the house seems inconvenient. Keep in mind that you won't have to do it for long and it will prevent a feeling of tension and frustration between you and your daughter.

Q: *She is not the kind of kid who will sit on my lap. I run after her trying to read her a book. She fusses and gets down immediately. How will I ever read to her?*

A: At this age if she is not interested in sitting down to read with you, don't force it. She will hear you reading to her sister, and she is hearing the rhythm of the words even if she doesn't seem to be paying attention. Be creative. Notice what engages her. Find stories that make her laugh. Try reading her a story while she is riding in the car or while she is in the bathtub. Enjoy the process of learning what grabs her attention and what makes her light up.

Q: *When I am trying to do something with my six-year-old, like stringing beads, the little one just throws them across the room. I can't put everything away. She is so physical! She is making me and my older daughter crazy!*

A: Set time aside with your six-year-old when the toddler is sleeping, hire a babysitter or ask your spouse to play with the little one so you and your eldest can have time alone. When the toddler is with you, put the beads away. You have to set up your environment so that you are not feeling antagonistic all the time. That will eventually hurt your relationship with her. Your frustration is only going to make her realize that the time she gets the most reaction and attention from you is when she is acting the wildest.

Q: *So do I ignore the throwing beads?*

A: No. If you ignore a behavior, it is sure to escalate, and it sends a message that it is alright to act out. Pick her up and have her help clean up the mess in whatever way she can.

Now, tell the six-year-old that you will do quiet things with her when her sister is napping or with dad. When the three of you are together you will all be doing activities that the youngest can participate in successfully, e.g. going out for a hike, putting on a puppet show or doing aerobic dances. Find an avenue for the young one to release energy and direct her energy in a positive way instead of asking her to conform to a setting that she is still not capable of handling. Find things the three of you can do successfully together and have fun. Then get those beads out when the toddler is asleep.

By thinking of activities that she can participate in, you avoid conflict and frustration for all three of you. You won't have to rearrange your schedule for long; before you know it she will be six years old.

Q: *But will she ever be able to go to school and listen?*

A: Of course! She is only fifteen months old. She is just traveling a different path than the one you have experienced with your first-born. Her kinesthetic exploration is showing you her wonderful, creative, investigative brain. That is good. It is different than what you are used to, but our job as parents is to let each unique personality blossom. Don't worry about her academics at this point. That will come. She just needs to feel loved and accepted.

Enjoy both your daughters and celebrate their differences.

****

Q: *My eighteen-month-old son has a hot temper and throws tantrums, what do I do?*

A: His tantrum is a technique he uses to try to get his way. Pick a time when he is calm and not emotional to explain to him that when he wants something from you, he needs to ask in a polite voice. Let him know that you are interested in his feelings and needs, but he must communicate those needs without being rude. Tell him that, from now on, if he decides to throw a fit, you will move away from him and not speak to him until he quiets down and stops the tantrum. There is nothing to be gained by trying to talk to a child in the midst of a temper tantrum.

A tantrum is rude and unacceptable so you must be very consistent about not getting roped into dialogue with him when he is full of temper. Walk away. Wait to start a conversation when he is calm.

You might also give him a special pillow. Tell him, "I know that sometimes you feel so frustrated and mad. When that happens, instead of screaming and crying please go into your room and yell into or pound on this pillow until your anger quiets down and then come back and talk to me in a calm voice."

However, in some cases, once a tantrum escalates, your son may simply lose control and you can help him by holding him tight. While you hold him, even though he may be kicking and flailing his arms about, remain very calm and say nothing. Keep holding him until the temper is over. Eventually he will quiet. Anger management is a crucial skill, but he is very young now and may still need you to intervene. As he gets older, helping him find ways to notice his temper before it spirals out of control will be very important.

In each of these cases, by removing yourself verbally or physically from your child during his tantrum, you are teaching him that the tantrum gains no reward.

Tantrums are only successful if they get lots of attention and a parent gives in to the child's demands. When your son realizes his temper does not achieve successful results, the technique of the tantrum will be abandoned.

****

Q: *My child is not nice to our animals. She is going on two. Why is she so mean? Her older brother was never mean like this.*

A: Be sure that your animals are safe. Do not leave them in the room with your child if you think they could get hurt. At her age, your daughter needs to be chaperoned when she is with an animal or with another child. She is in the age of investigation by touch. Her job right now is to explore, poke, push, taste, and touch everything.

Keep the animals in a place where you can pet them with her, and where the animals will be safely tucked away from her if you are not there. Set good examples by demonstrating how to handle the animal and congratulate her when she is gentle. If she becomes rough, remove her or the animal and state simply that she does not get the privilege of being with the animal if she is rough. The same rule would apply to her being rough with another child.

Chapter 13:
She is In My Stuff!

Q: *My three-year-old is driving me nuts! She is touching all of my stuff. I have knick knacks on my coffee table and end tables that are mine and she knows that, yet she still moves them around and sometimes breaks something. These are my things, she has her own toys, and I want her to leave my stuff alone! I spank her, I put her in her room, I scream, and nothing works.*

A: Your daughter's job at the age of three is to explore everything. She is supposed to touch, look, hear, feel and see what the world is made up of — everything is under investigation.

Were she fourteen I would have a much different answer for you. But at three, you are setting yourself up for a constant battle and an unpleasant relationship with your child by leaving your special items out. Find a high shelf or cupboard where these things can be stored for a few years until she can understand the concepts of 'personal' and 'fragile'. Leave things out that you don't mind letting her touch and move.

You may not like the idea of changing your decor for your child, but if you take a step back you can see that by compromising you will avoid conflict. This is not "giving in" to your daughter. It is only temporary remodeling. She is very young and you are simply organizing her environment so that you and she can build a positive relationship instead of being immersed in negativity much of the day.

Let her do the important job of a three-year-old and explore everything she can reach. Instead of being frustrated that you have to rearrange for a while, be thrilled that by putting away valuable items, you have just prevented daily stress and conflicts in your house.

Chapter 14:
Jealous of the Baby

Q: *My daughter, who is three, has become very clingy and weepy since the baby arrived. She will not leave my side. She will not go with her dad, she will not play with other kids, and she will not go to her school that she loves. I don't know what to do. She screams and kicks if I try to get her to go someplace. I can't take it. I have tried threats, bribes and tears. Nothing works.*

A: It is so common for children to react strongly to a big change in the family. Family is the one constant that children depend on as they venture out to explore the ever-changing world around them. The unknown is scary and they just want the old familiar routine back.

There are many triggers that could have made your daughter feel insecure about being away from you now. It could be simply that you went to the hospital, or that you look different, or that your time is divided now, or that you act different because you are sleep deprived. Whatever the cause, she needs time to adjust to the changes in her life.

In order to help her feel comfortable and capable, take small steps. For example, take her to a place like Grandma's or her school where she knows the environment and likes it. Stay with her a little while until she is engaging in activities. Then tell her you are just going out to the car to get your book. Come right back, so she knows that when you leave, it is temporary. Even if she cries when you leave, she needs to see that she can indeed cope. The hardest part is, when you leave her, if she is screaming at you and kicking, try very hard not to react. Just remain calm and continue doing what you are doing. Tell her you love her and you will be back in 15 minutes. Don't exhibit frustration and don't cry. Be calm and steady so she sees that you are fine. She trusts you and your body language will tell her a lot. If you stick to it and stay calm, she will adjust to the change in the family and realize that her world is still safe and good.

****

Q: *My son will not stop harassing his sister. Every time he walks by he jabs her. Every time she comes near him he hits her with a toy. She is two years old and he is five. He was fine with her the first year, but now I am really afraid he is going to seriously hurt her. He pulls her hair, hits her face, yanks her arm and knocks her down.*

A: Because of the imminent danger here, this is one behavior that needs to be addressed with absolute consistency, 24/7. Do not let it slide another day.

Because the behavior is continuing, whatever you are doing is not making an impact on your son. He needs to learn self-control so he will not hurt her and will not alienate people in his future.

If he is being aggressive, remove him or your daughter from the room right away. Put him in the next room separated by a door gate so he can still see you. Let him play alone for a few minutes then when he calms down, if he wants to come back in and try again, great, but the minute the aggression shows, remove one of them. The consequence has to be immediate isolation. The concept is: 'If you are mean to people, you don't get to be with people'.

If you are working or cooking and feel that you cannot watch them closely, put her in a backpack or another safe place separate from her brother so it will not be an issue.

When you have time to watch closely and you are all together, if five minutes go by with him playing kindly, make a huge deal out of it. Talk about how fabulous it is when you can all play together and be kind to each other. Tell him that it is so wonderful when he is gentle and shares. Take every opportunity to give him positive attention in the good times.

Any time he shows aggression, repeat to him, "You are hurting your sister. I am taking her out of this room because it is my job to keep you both safe. I will not let her hurt you, and I will not let you hurt her. I know that you are capable of playing gently with her. If you want to try playing with her again let me know and we will come back and play when you are ready to be gentle." Put it in his hands so he realizes he needs to play nicely if he wants to interact with others.

Ultimately, if he treats other people with aggression, he will be rejected by kids in general; that is the natural consequence. So work very hard to congratulate him when he is interacting successfully so that he starts to focus on the positive behaviors. Notice every small moment that he cooperates, or plays calmly. Catch him in the act of being good as often as possible. See if you can strategically end playtime on a good note before he gets aggressive, so the playing was a positive experience.

Also be sure to spend individual time with him so he can relax and not have to deal at all with his sister and has your undivided attention. Tell him that at noon you have hired a sitter for his sister because you want to have some time alone with him. He will see that you value his feelings and you are making a special effort to be with him.

****

Q: *I tell my three-year-old daughter that she has to be gentle with the baby and she always says, "I am" while she is poking her finger into his face. How do I make her understand?*

A: Take the time to show her different ways to be gentle with a doll. Ask her to imagine a bunny rabbit, how soft it is and how softly you would pet his fur. Or give her a stuffed animal and see if she can pet it without squishing its hair. Tell her that the baby is not big and strong yet like her and that when she was little, you asked everyone to be gentle with her too.

Sometimes, if she seems to be getting a little too rough but it is clearly unintentional, just pick the baby up and distract your eldest with another activity, so that her whole day is not filled with conversation centered on being good to the baby. Often, just by the sheer necessities of dealing with a newborn, the older siblings feel that all your time is focused on that baby. Give her time to be alone with you. During those times that you are all together, talk about her as the big sister and all her abilities. Congratulate her each time she touches the baby with a gentle hand. Involve her in ways that make her feel important and loved. You need to be sure to make it obvious that you have time for both children and enough love to go around.

****

Q: *What about my four-year-old who is manipulating me? He tells me that he doesn't want to go to his friend's anymore. At night he says he is scared. When I ask him to go to sleep he says it is not fair that the baby doesn't have to go to sleep. Usually, it is just easier to lie down with him instead of dealing with trying to get him to lie down alone and be independent. But my husband thinks I am letting him control me. I'm concerned that sometimes he can't separate from me; maybe I haven't done such a great job of fostering his independence.*

A: No, no. Please don't judge your parenting skills by your child's behavior after the arrival of a sibling! His whole world has just been reshaped and is confusing. The routine is changing and daily life is not as familiar and consistent as it once was for him.

At his age, do not worry about attachment and certainly not about sleeping alone. It is just fine to let him sleep with you if you are comfortable with that, or sit beside his bed until he falls asleep. If you don't lie down with him and he is not getting to bed until 10 p.m. then you both are exhausted and frustrated – so lie down with him and let bedtime be easy and calm. Meet his need for comfort and slowly work at moving towards independence by sitting next to him or sitting in the next room.

Take him to friends' houses and stay with him so he can play and know that you are not going to disappear with the baby. After a number of times, try telling him that you'll stay a little while and then you need to run to the grocery and you'll come right back and pick him up. Remind him that he is so lucky he is big enough to stay and play with a friend, while his baby sister has to go to the grocery because she is too small to play.

Give it time. He will get comfortable in the new routine of chaos which comes with multiple children and he will want his independence back. Just let him know he is safe and you love him, and time will get you all through this.

****

Q: *Ever since our baby arrived, when I tell my oldest daughter not to do something, she says, "You don't love me anymore". She complains that I don't love her because I don't pick her up anymore! Then I feel guilty and give her sweets or extra time on the TV. Is this emotional blackmail by a four-year-old?!*

A: As parents, we are emotionally charged creatures. When a young child says, "You don't love me", we feel responsible and worry that we have ruined her for life! In reality she is finding a way to get your attention.

With the arrival of a sibling, your job is to find a positive way to give attention to your eldest child. In the middle of a busy day, take just a moment for no reason to hold her and tell her that you love her. Try to schedule time to be alone with her. When the baby is sleeping, even though you want to get caught up on chores, take some of that time to play alone with your daughter. Plan a 'big girls' evening while another adult watches the baby. It is easy to forget how important it is to her to have time alone with you and not have to share you with the baby every minute of the day.

Don't let her "I am unloved" dialogue control you in a busy moment. Do not offer her treats which reinforce her dramatic performance. Just stay calm and matter of fact. Tell her that indeed you do love her and that you would love to sit, snuggle and read with her as soon as dinner is finished.

Chapter 15: Screaming Tot

Q: *When I bring my four-year-old son to preschool, I carry my two-year-old in, put him down and let him play a while. When it is time for my toddler and me to leave the school and we say good bye to his brother, he screams as loud as he can all the way out to the car. I am so tired and embarrassed by his screaming. Sometimes I let him play longer, thinking he will feel he had enough time to play, but whenever we leave, no matter how long I let him play, he screams.*

A: Once you have picked him up to leave, don't put him down.

Explain to him, at home when he is calm that next time you drop off his brother at preschool, you will not be letting him play because he screams when you leave and that is not acceptable behavior. However, the second day you go, you will let him play if he agrees not to scream when you leave.

When you bring him the first time, he will undoubtedly fuss and struggle in your arms, just remind him that he cannot play today but he can try again next time.

The following day, remind him of the rule: he gets to play as long as he does not scream upon leaving. If he manages to hold up his end of the bargain, thank him profusely, congratulate him on his grown up behavior and mention that next time it will be great knowing that he gets to play again.

If he screams or fusses when you leave, pick him up and go to the car. Do not give him a few more minutes! Do not talk. Wait quietly for him to finish crying. Then tell him calmly that since he started screaming when it was time to leave, you will not let him play the next two times you go to school and he can try again on the third time.

Keep giving him chances, with the acceptable behavior explained very clearly.

By giving him the responsibility of managing himself appropriately, you provide him with an opportunity to learn self-discipline and build self-confidence as he realizes that he really can manage his own behavior.

Chapter 16:
But He Doesn't Have To!

Q: *My daughter is confused by other kids' behavior and says, "Mom, that kid is jumping on the bed and his mom says it is ok, so why can't I jump on the bed too?"*

A: Sit down with your daughter and explain that every family has different sets of rules. "There are certain activities that we may think are inappropriate while other families are accepting of those same activities. For instance, some parents let their children eat ice cream before dinner, in our family that is not something we do. All families are different and that is good. Wherever you go, you will meet people who have different rules than you, but *your* family rules go with you all the time. So, since it is not ok at our house to jump on the beds, then you should not jump on the beds at someone else's house either. In our opinion, beds are built to sleep on, they are not built to jump on. I would like you to do your jumping on a tramp or pogo stick."

Throughout your child's life she will see behavior that is intriguing to her. At this early age you can build the foundation for helping your child realize as a teenager that if her friends are smoking, she can choose not to participate. Let your daughter know that she can function in a different home and with a variety of friends. Remind her that she does not have to do everything they do and she can still have fun. "It is fine for every family to have different rules, it is quite interesting, but remember the rules of your family and wherever you go they go with you."

****

Q: *My son gets upset at the park when I discipline him for throwing sand. He sees other children who do not get disciplined for the same behavior. He has a tantrum and says I am mean and that I don't like him. He is five years old.*

A: Don't say much at the park because it is too hard for any of us to listen when we are emotional. Simply tell him it is time to go, or that you and he are going to take a walk. Then, when he has calmed down, explain to him, "I need you to know that the rules that we have in our family go wherever we go. The reason we don't throw sand is because it could get in someone's eyes and really hurt them. I didn't make that rule to be mean, and I love you, and I know you can remember to use sand for digging and building but not for throwing. What other parents tell their children is up to them, but whether you are at the park or at a friend's house, I do not want you throwing sand." Then let him know you would be happy to go back to the park and let him play. Tell him you feel confident that he can remember not to throw sand. It is always important to let children try again and know that you believe in their ability to learn form their mistakes.

Four to six years old

Your smile
Your sparkling eyes
Your tears
Your voice

No one else
Has these things

No one else
Does what you do
No one else
Is exactly the same

Rejoice
In your difference

Chapter 17: Pretend Play

Q: *When do we tell our kids what is real and what is fantasy? My son, four years old, thinks he is Captain Hook and he loves pretending that all day. Do I have to break that fantasy?*

A: No. Pretend play is a fantastic way for children to sort through many social concepts and to be creative.

You might want to talk about Hook's behavior. Suggest to your son that he may want to remind Hook of the rules of your house while he is living there, such as, 1) he may use his sword only when he is on his ship, never in the house, and you live in a house, but perhaps the bathtub would be a safe place to imagine you are on a ship, and 2) he needs to be very careful of his hook so that it does not get caught on anything or bump anyone.

Your son is being creative and imaginative. If there are no inappropriate behaviors stemming from that pretend play, then there is no reason to squelch it.

****

Q: My daughter, who is five, insists that we set a place at the dinner table for her imaginary friend. Is there something wrong with her?

A: Not at all, she is using great creativity and imagination and should be allowed to do so.

Set an extra place and see what the friend has to offer to the dinner table conversation. She might tell you things your daughter would be reluctant to discuss, or she might open the door for a better understanding of your daughter's feelings.

Or she might just be comforting to your daughter. If, by chance, the imaginary friend gets an attitude (i.e., your daughter trying out behaviors without really taking the responsibility) tell your daughter to teach her friend the rules of the house. Otherwise her friend won't be welcome at the table.

Chapter 18: Talking Back

Q: *What do I do when my four-year-old son informs me that he is having M&Ms for breakfast? I say to him, "No, you are not having M&Ms for breakfast," and he says, "Yes, I am having M&Ms for breakfast," and I say, "No, you are not having M&Ms for breakfast. They are not good for you," and that goes on until he leaves for preschool at 9:00. I finally did give him two M&Ms because he had eaten his regular breakfast while we were arguing.*

A: HE WON! Those two M&Ms let him know that the battle is worth fighting! Every time you give in and give him 2 M&Ms, he will push harder the next time. Their persistence is unbelievable. The fact is, if you say "no" to something eight times, and then you say "yes," the next time he will ask sixteen times. Just say "no" and be done.

Do not engage in verbal power struggles with your child. It is never productive and usually leads to heightened emotion and frustration, which leads to anger. Sometimes we, as parents, think we need to justify and explain our decisions and we get engaged in these yes/no arguments that make us crazy and accomplish nothing. The bottom line is - Don't go there!

Simply reply the first time, "I will never serve M&Ms for breakfast, not ever, and I am not talking to you about this anymore. M&Ms are not breakfast food." If he continues to argue, ignore him or tell him you would like him to go in the other room because he is bothering you and you will not talk about this any more. Quite literally, stop talking to him. If you do not respond, eventually he will stop because there is no reaction.

No matter how annoying he is, take a breath and say nothing. This calmly and clearly shows him that his nagging is fruitless and he gets zero attention so there is no motivation for him to keep it up.

Subjects like this need to be black and white for children. If it is never ok and never going to be OK, then be sure you never give in. As soon as we let it be gray, and perhaps give in once, they will push and push relentlessly.

Note: Don't kick yourself for giving in. We all make mistakes. Do not be hard on yourself, be proud that you have noticed the problem and want to learn. Some kids are so good at engaging us in these battles that we are already in it before we realize what has happened. Just stop when you see what is going on and end the conversation.

****

Q: *When I tell my son it is time to leave, he says, in a rude tone of voice, "I'm not going! And you can't make me!" I yell back and say it is time to go now! He still doesn't listen and I end up waiting longer and then we are late.*

A: If this is a regular pattern of behavior, the first thing to do is to have a conversation at some quiet time when you are just hanging out together. Say to him that you have noticed that he is having a hard time when you say it is time to go. Tell him that it is unacceptable to speak to you in a rude voice and that you will no longer respond to that voice. From now on when you tell him it is time to go, you expect him to cooperate and speak to you politely if he has anything to say. Explain that you have decided that you will give him a five-minute warning so he can wrap up what he is doing and then when the five minutes are up, if he cannot manage to leave on his own, you will have no discussion, but you will pick him up and leave.

When the time comes, if he refuses to cooperate and/or uses a crabby voice, just pick him up and go. No dialogue. Do not engage in an argument with him. Just leave with him in your arms. If he is in his PJ's, then bring his clothes along, and dress him later in the car.

Our temptation is to engage in verbal battle when everybody is charged - you're arguing – your voice escalates - he has already tuned you out - nothing is going to be accomplished when emotions are already high.

Have a rational conversation with him when he is calm. Tell him the rules. Let him know that there will be times when he will be able to make choices and other times when he needs to go along with the family plan. But in either case, when he speaks to you to tell you his opinion, he must use a pleasant tone of voice. Be sure that you speak to him politely as well. If children get the information when they are calm, and it is explained in a way that makes sense to them, they will remember the rules and be more cooperative. No one listens or retains information when he is angry or frustrated.

Chapter 19:
Discipline is Not Working

Q: *Lately I have had to ask my four-year-old to brush her teeth at least twelve times before she does so. I tell her about the natural consequence of not brushing, which would be bad breath and rotten teeth, but she doesn't care about that.*

A: Those natural consequences are very abstract concepts for a four-year-old.

There are some things at this age that are just non-negotiable. Personal hygiene is one of them because it is crucial to healthy life.

First I would sit down and talk to her when she is calm and there is no argument going on. Tell her what is going to happen from now on. Tell her that you have explained how important it is to brush your teeth and that, "I am only going to ask once from now on. It doesn't matter to me if you like to do it or not. My job as your mom is to teach you to keep your teeth healthy. So I am going to do my job. I will give you a five-minute warning and then when I ask you to brush, I will expect you to do that. If not, I will be picking you up and taking you into the bathroom and brushing them myself."

Later, when it is time for her to brush her teeth, give her the five-minute warning. In five minutes it will be time to stop what she is doing and brush her teeth. When the five minutes are up tell her it is time to brush. If she does not respond, pick her up, carry her to the bathroom and place her in front of the sink. If you must, put the toothbrush in her hand and brush her teeth with her to get the job done. Then thank her for brushing.

Kids need limits. If they get away with a certain behavior, you can be sure they will repeat it. If you ask her twelve times and she doesn't budge and no one makes her go, she knows there will be no consequence. If it takes twelve times now, it will take fifteen or twenty times next week when she is involved in something really interesting. So instead of allowing your temper to escalate with each request and thus teaching her to ignore you, simply and calmly pick her up after the first request. Eliminate the struggle altogether.

There are some topics where there just is no room for argument (i.e. you don't touch the hot stove, you don't bite people and you do brush your teeth).

****

Q: *In our house, we come in the door and take our shoes off; that's a family rule. Our four-year-old daughter knows this. She has been doing it for years. Now, all of a sudden, she is walking through the house with shoes on. And she walks on the couch now! When I yell at her, she laughs and gets off, so I know she knows it is wrong.*

A: She is investigating how much power she has.

She knows the rule. Now she has decided to test it. This will happen throughout child rearing. There will be a plateau when you think you have gotten through to them, and then suddenly they will test what you thought was already understood.

If she is climbing on the furniture, it is most effective just to pick her up and skip the emotional and lengthy inquisition about what she is up to – she knows not to walk on the couch, she is just trying it out, so pick her up and remind her that it is absolutely unacceptable to walk on furniture.

When she walks in the door, try to be right there to greet her and if she starts to walk into the house, pick her up and set her back at the doorway and ask her what the rule is about shoes.

Your voice, though calm, should get firmer each time she breaks a rule. Explain to her that it is unacceptable to do this, "I have asked you twice not to stand on the couch, and if it happens again you will have to stay next to me and not play in the living room for a while." Or, "I'm not having a discussion about this; it is never ok to walk on the couch. If you are having trouble remembering that rule, then stay in the kitchen with me and play in here."

Part of it is attention getting: you may be busy at your desk or on the phone, and she is thinking, "I know how to get her to see me - I'll stand on the couch!" At the age of four, cause and effect are making sense! Be aware of how much or little time you are spending interacting with her and suggest perhaps that she can help you at your desk. Tell her that you appreciate her playing on her own and when the timer goes off in thirty minutes, you will be happy to play a game.

One of the hardest parts of parenting is to be there all the time. It is especially hard when you are in the middle of something that needs your full attention, like cooking dinner. Those are the moments when children most easily get away with breaking the rules. It is so important for you to try to stay tuned in to your children and address the behavior issue the moment it occurs. Make a big effort to be there at the moment of the infraction so you can tell her immediately what needs to happen, and then enforce a consequence if need be.

****

Q: *I'm constantly saying, "Don't do this, don't do that." I feel like I have to nag all day long. "Don't push, don't throw toys, pick up your clothes, use your fork..."*

A: It does get tiring for us as adults to have to keep repeating the same rules over and over. But the pay-off is huge if we hang in there. You do indeed have to spend a good deal of time correcting inappropriate behavior, so balance that by congratulating your children for every little positive action.

Be prompt in thanking them every time they do something nice or thoughtful and tell them how proud they should be of their behavior. "This has been so pleasant," or "Boy, what a great way to ask," "Thank you for remembering to walk," "Thank you for picking up that spoon."

In between the frequent reminders of desired behavior, show them that you are noticing when they share, when they ask politely for something, when they help out without being asked.

It's all about consideration and respect towards other people. That's why we work so hard. And the rewards are so huge.

****

Q: *My son, who is four, likes to throw books across the floor because he knows it upsets me. I usually take privileges away; for instance, I won't let him watch his favorite TV show, but it doesn't seem to be working.*

A: Consequences need to have some meaningful connection with the infraction. Not watching TV is a punishment that has nothing to do with the inappropriate behavior of throwing a book. In general, random punishments do not work. They are about control and power, not about helping the child learn.

Let's say your son threw a book across the room. At first, point out that the behavior is not acceptable and what needs to be done about it. "Books are for reading, not throwing. You need to set the book back on the shelf."

Then let him go back and try again. Always, always, let him go try again. Let him know you have the faith in him that he can use books correctly. Two minutes later, if the book is across the floor again, go pick him up and address it again. "Now I will ask you to stay away from the books for a while. We can read later when you are ready to handle the books appropriately." (Please do not underestimate the ability of your child to understand long words!)

The crucial thing is that you address the issue immediately. Do not think, "Oh, I am baking, I will go deal with it in a few minutes." After a few minutes, he knows that he got away with inappropriate behavior and he will try that again since it was successful.

Q: *What if you tell him to go pick up the book and he says "no"?*

A: If you ask him to pick up the book and he refuses, tell him that when he has picked up the book, you will play a game with him. He can sit on the couch by himself until he is ready to do so. Some children may choose to sit there for quite a while. That is ok. Be sure you put him on a couch or stair where there is nothing to do and nothing to fiddle with. If he is on the stairs squirming, just ignore it. When he fusses on the couch or stairs and makes faces, he is doing that just to get a reaction. If you ignore it, you are taking the reward out of it for him. In a few minutes, go back to him and say, "Thank you for sitting here, would you like to go with me to pick up that book now and then we can do that great puzzle?"

Stand your ground. Don't give in and do it yourself. Some children are far more willful than others. After a while, if he is still sitting being stubborn, you can simply pick him up and go get the book, put it in his hand, and help him set it on the shelf. Thank him for picking up the book. You got the job done, and you can move on. He will have learned that he cannot ignore your requests and that you don't lose your cool or give up. If we say no ten times and then give in on the eleventh time, then the next time he will try twenty five times waiting for the time you'll give in. We cannot give in.

We all have different guidelines of what we will accept and what we will not. Explain what you want him to do, wait a few minutes, then go back to him and offer to go with him to do what you asked. Often offering to go with your child is key, because it is a lot to expect of a four-year-old to be sitting on the couch and think, "I messed up and I better get up and go fix it." If he is on the couch and realizes he made an error and then you offer to help him rectify it, it is easier for him to see what he should be doing. You have to remember to look closely at what you are expecting of him at this age.

It is so important that we reward every attempt a child makes to do the right thing. Show him that he made the right choice by helping you pick up and the struggle is over. Always try to find that moment when you see him make an effort to do the right thing and tell him what a great a job he is doing. Next time he will be more likely to do the right thing faster.

And remember, instead of taking away unrelated privileges, provide immediate action directly related to what he is doing.

****

Q: *I have a four-year-old son who is really good at getting into mischief. He will take off out the back door running and never look back or go quietly into the bedroom and draw all over the sheets with marker. I have read every book and tried every discipline technique. I yell all day, I try time outs, and then I just give up.*

A: You actually just answered your question. You try something, and then give up.

Some children are born with personalities that can cope with the inconsistencies of our parenting. Others are genetically wired in such a way that they require clarity and consistency. Without that consistency, they don't know what to do, and may become agitated. Our inconsistency makes them feel that they cannot trust us to keep them safe.

You may have a son who quite seriously cannot manage the fact that sometimes you scream at him and sometimes you do nothing. It may make him feel totally insecure and confused. He may be trying whatever he can to get you to focus and draw the line for him.

For all children, a consequence has to be of some value to the child or it is ineffective. It has to mean something to them personally, so they do not want to repeat the action that will have that consequence. Constant yelling is not a consequence many kids care about. They just learn to tune it out. So usually you find yourself yelling more and more as they turn a deaf ear, not caring.

You say you have tried everything. I wonder if you have been consistent when you have tried things. Using a time-out, for example. If you use it once or five times, but the sixth time you let it go and gave up, then you just taught him to misbehave seven or eight times because surely you'll give up.

It seems that your son is highly creative and values his independence. You might try telling him that you love him and that it is your job to keep him safe. Therefore, the next time he behaves inappropriately, you will be coming up to him, taking his hand and keeping him attached to your side until you decide you are ready to let him try again to be independent and use his own good judgment.

He will not like it. But if you stick to it, never give up, and keep him with you, you are taking away his freedom and he may just decide that is a consequence he does not want repeated. You must stick with it. It may take ten times every five minutes, or 400 times throughout a day. But finally he will see that you are dead serious and are never going to give up, and then he will trust in you, change his attitude and start to think before he acts.

Chapter 20:
Scared at Night

Q: *My daughter is four and cannot go to sleep in her own room. I read parenting books and I am afraid she won't have confidence in herself if she can't go to sleep alone. I don't know how to get her to sleep without me in the room. She always says she is scared. If I tell her to be a big girl and that I know she can do it, the crying goes on and on and none of us get to sleep.*

A: Think of all the things she does do on her own - getting herself dressed, helping you set the table, brushing her teeth - it sounds like you are giving her ample opportunity to feel self-confident and capable. Don't let bedtime be a struggle for anyone.

Be consistent about the bedtime ritual. Find a pattern that works for your child and the whole family, and do it consistently. If it means lying down with her, or sitting in a chair in the next room so she can see you, or reading a story and letting her fall asleep to the sound of your voice, or singing to her, do it. Make her feel safe. At this young age, fear of the dark is instinctual. With time and patience, she will feel safe enough to tackle it on her own knowing that you have always been there and will continue to be so even if she can't see you.

Chapter 21:
Restaurant Behavior

Q: *I took my son out to lunch after preschool and he was all over the place. How much is too much nagging? I mean, he wasn't awful, but every 30 seconds I kept saying, "Ok sit down, come back and sit down, get up off the floor and sit down." I want to be chatting with my friends and instead I am constantly nagging him.*

A: The fact that you are nagging him every 30 seconds means... he wins!

He gets your attention. And his behavior does not change. Don't nag him. Tell him that in a restaurant we sit in our chairs and if he cannot do that you will take him home. Then do it - leave and take him home.

That's the hard part, because the selfish side of us wants to be able to have lunch and relax and chat with our friends. But once a parent, we have to let go of those selfish wants, and address the issue with our child. That is the job we accepted when we became a parent. (Sometimes take a break from your job of parenting and arrange to go out alone with friends).

At this age, eating out is a time to teach your child how to act appropriately in a restaurant. Before you go, explain to him the rules of eating out and how much fun it is to go out to eat with friends. Tell him that you will bring crayons and paper along or a small toy for him to play with quietly while you wait for the food. Remind him that he needs to remain seated and use a quiet voice. When he is in the restaurant with you and managing well for a few minutes, turn to him and congratulate him: "Wow, thanks for sitting so nicely, it is very fun to bring you to the restaurant." If you are with friends, be sure to interrupt your own conversation to include your child from time to time and ask him about his day or what his favorite movie is. On your way home thank him for trying so hard to remember his good manners and tell him he will get to go with you next time you go out.

On the other hand, if his behavior is disruptive and he cannot act appropriately, you must forfeit your own desire to eat out with your friends and tell them you would love to try again next week. Get your food to go and take him out of the restaurant. Explain in the car that because he could not use his good manners, the lunch is over and next week when you go out, he will be staying home with a baby sitter. Next time you go, remind him why he is not going with you. Then also assure him that you are confident that he is capable of appropriate restaurant behavior and he will be able to come with you and try again the next time.

With some positive feedback from you, and a few opportunities, your child will quickly learn that eating out is fun and will learn his restaurant manners.

Note: Please be considerate of your child in choosing the places you take him. Don't expect a preschooler to sit through a four-course meal. Let him know that different restaurants require different behaviors. If you are at Small World Play-A-Lot, it's ok to be active and loud. Let him know that there are lots of other kids there and that the reason parents come is to let their kids play. However, if you are at a nice restaurant, he can also understand that people in that type of restaurant want to be able to have a relaxing dinner talking with each other and do not like to be interrupted by a loud child.

A child's attention span is short, but that will lengthen with time! For now, your expectations need to be realistic for his age. Realize that he will be done eating quickly and sitting still is an effort. Bring quiet toys and be prepared to take the rest of your meal to go if it means you can leave on a positive note.

Chapter 22:
Tears and Anger

Q: *Just in the past two months, my daughter, six-years-old, has begun getting angry very quickly and falling into tears as soon as we try to address her behavior. She is a wreck about five times a day. It is exhausting and I can't take the screaming and hysterical tears any more. Why did this happen? What is causing her intense emotions and why is she so mad?*

A: You may or may not ever find out the answer to those questions. But what you can do is help her learn to handle those strong emotions in an appropriate way.

Be sure to acknowledge her feelings with compassion; don't degrade her or belittle her feelings. Let her know that you understand she is frustrated or annoyed, but that in any event, yelling or kicking is not acceptable behavior. Explain that any time she is feeling angry or frustrated with a person or situation, she has the choice to walk away instead of lashing out.

Tell her again and again that she can manage her feelings by walking away and avoiding inappropriate behavior instead of getting in trouble for engaging in such behavior. She is capable of making the choice of walking away and letting herself cool down before talking to anyone. (Don't we wish many thirty-year-olds had learned this skill?)

Explain to her in a moment of calm, that sometimes lately you see that she is feeling angry, and that when she feels that anger in her body, she should walk to a place where she can calm down. If she has trouble doing that, tell her you will come over and pick her up and set her someplace safe where she can calm down. There needn't be discussion at the time, simply pick her up and remove her from the situation. By doing this, you are showing her how that choice works, by helping her walk away. Avoid engaging in any dialogue that may escalate and become ineffective.

When your children are emotional, it is not the time to have discussions about their behavior. They get more intense, we get frustrated, and nothing positive is accomplished. Some children, not consciously at this age, love the effect of verbal conflict. They get a rise out of you and they are interested in seeing their effect on you. By gently lifting them up and removing them from the situation without dialogue, you take away their fuel for the fire. Without dialogue from you, they cannot engage in verbal battle.

Often when our kids get into these stages of high drama, they really cannot see a way out. They need us to help them notice and experience the appropriate behavior. Once you have tried this behavior modification, you might be surprised that the fits of rage and tears stop. Be proud that you have given your child a skill that will be a gift for the rest of her life. However, if the temper continues, then you might choose to seek help from an appropriate professional.

Chapter 23:
The Death of a Grandparent

Q: *I took my five-year-old to visit her sick grandma and her grandma unexpectedly died while we were there. It was very peaceful. Grandma just went to sleep. Since then my daughter doesn't want the lights out at night, doesn't want to go to school, and wants to sleep with me. Last night she was sobbing and I asked her if anything hurt or what was wrong, and she said she just didn't know why she was crying. This is a child who usually is very strong, independent and has never had trouble sleeping before. I am afraid I have done serious damage by having her witness the death.*

A: Whether or not your daughter was in the room, a very prominent person in her life has just disappeared from her life. She doesn't understand why and she doesn't know what caused the disappearance, all she knows is that she better hang on tight to those who are left.

Young children often do not know consciously what is causing their distress, but it is important for us to recognize their new fears and insecurities and acknowledge them. We can help our children learn to deal with them, regardless of the cause.

I would get her a cool new night light, like a lava lamp, which will grab her interest and divert her thoughts at bedtime. This will also let her know you respect her feelings and are happy to help by getting a nightlight. If she needs to sleep with you, I would let her. If you are not comfortable with that, you could put a sleeping bag next to your bed and let her sleep there, or stay in her room until she falls asleep. She just needs to feel certain that no one else will disappear if she goes to sleep. Tell her she has to go to school, but you will be there when she gets home, and you know she will have a great time with her friends at school. Let the teacher know your daughter's grandma died so the teacher can be a little extra attentive to, and patient with, the situation.

It is true that time heals and this too shall pass. Give her time and respect her feelings and as the days go by her fears will lessen. Don't feel frustrated that she has "regressed" in her independence. Accept her feelings and wait for her to return to her comfortable self – she will.

There are some fabulous books about dying that can be helpful to young children, such as <u>The Fall of Freddie the Leaf</u> or <u>Ten Best Things about Barney.</u> Consult your librarian.

Chapter 24:
Interrupting

Q: *My five-year-old has so many ways of interrupting. He just starts talking, or he bangs his feet together or he hits himself in the head – anything to get attention! I tell him to stop, over and over, but he just keeps it up. I'm not sure he even knows he is doing it anymore. Nothing I say can make it stop!*

A: You just answered that one: nothing you SAY can make it stop.

Now you have to DO something.

It sounds as if this has been going on for some time. Most likely, the reason there has been no improvement is that there has been no consequence, just a lot of talk.

I would tell your son that you realize that you have not taught him that it is inappropriate to interrupt and that you will be implementing a new technique starting now. If he interrupts, with words or sounds, you will politely ask him to stop. If he cooperates, please make a conscious effort to pause after just a few minutes, thank him for not interrupting and give him a chance to say what was on his mind. However, if it continues, pick him up, remove him from the area and say, "You need to stay away from us for a moment because you are interrupting and that is rude to the person who is talking. I will come and get you in a few minutes and you can try again." Go back to the conversation. In a few minutes you can invite your son to join you and ask him what he wanted to say.

Be calm. Be matter of fact. Be consistent. It works!

Chapter 25: Bullying at Four

Q: *There is a boy at my daughter's daycare center who is big trouble and is tormenting her. She has gone there since birth and she is now four. He just came this year, and he has it in for her. We have had conferences with the director and the teacher, but there have been no results. Our daughter comes home with bruises and scratches almost daily. My husband thinks she should be tough, take it and learn to defend herself. I wonder if I should still make her go there? I have told her to ignore the boy and perhaps the behavior will stop because there will be no reaction from her. She cries and says she doesn't want to go. Once she gets there the teachers say she keeps to herself and is close to tears all day. Should I be dumping my daughter somewhere she hates to be if I know there is room for her at another center? My husband says we are not giving in and she has to go.*

A: MOVE HER. She is only four-years-old. The rest of her life she will have to cope with different personalities and will have plenty of opportunity to learn to stand up for herself. But if she feels threatened and the school cannot resolve the problem effectively, you do not want to undermine her trust in you. You don't want to show disrespect for her feelings nor take the risk of personal injury. From the sound of it, this is truly a case of being bullied. Trust your instincts. No one knows your child as well as you do. If the bruises and scratches are not enough, you can go to the school and discreetly observe for a day or two to see exactly what is happening.

On some level, your husband is right. There is a time and place to learn to not allow someone to treat you badly, and we should encourage this concept from a very early age. However at the tender age of four, children still need interference from their parents on their behalf. She is so young and she relies on you to keep her safe. If you have the option of another center, there is no reason to keep your child in a situation in which she feels unsafe.

At four, children should be in a safe environment where they can concentrate on mastering social skills like sharing, using a polite voice, listening when someone else is talking, using scissors, showing compassion - and, yes, learning to stick up for themselves. They can learn this by telling another child not to grab, or not to cut in line, or not to knock over the block tower. But if your daughter is being physically harmed and emotionally scared, then it is time for the lioness instincts to come out. Take action and remove her from the dangerous situation.

Chapter 26: Baby Talk

Q: *My child, age five, is talking baby talk and it is driving me nuts!*

A: Kids are such mimickers and quick learners that if they hear a word or phrase once, they want to try it out. (That's one reason it is such a good time to teach them foreign languages!)

When you are having a quiet moment with your child, sit down and show her the difference between polite speech and baby talk. Speak the same sentence to her in a polite voice and then in baby talk and ask her which voice she likes. Tell her that she has a lovely grown up voice and that is the voice you would like to hear. Let her know that baby talk and whining are rude and from now on, if she chooses to use baby talk, you will not respond to her until she changes her voice.

The next time you hear a baby voice, calmly say, "I will listen to you when you remember to use your pleasant voice." Or, "Please say that again using a polite voice and then I will be happy to listen to you." Ignore the baby talk. If you walk away, she knows exactly why you are doing that. This is all part of helping her learn to be respectful, and teaching her that no one wants to do something for someone who is nagging or whining at them.

She'll stop because she will not like being ignored.

Note: It is essential that you use a polite voice when you speak to her and give her the same respect you are asking for from her. Children learn the fastest through role modeling. Use this to your advantage.

Chapter 27:
Son Won't Leave

Q: *Wherever we go, when I tell my five-year-old that it is time to leave, he says "No" and will not come with me. I don't want to make a scene in public so I usually tell him he can have two more minutes, but then when I say time is up, he still says "No." If I force the issue, he screams and embarrasses me, so I just let him keep playing.*

A: You just hit it on the head...he figured out how to get his way.

Your son has learned that when you are out you will not follow through, so he keeps telling you "No," knowing that there will be no consequence.

I would give him notice and tell him you will be leaving in five minutes, that you are glad he has been having such a good time and that when you come to get him to leave you expect him to cooperate.

In five minutes, walk over to where he is and tell him calmly that it is time to go. If he comes along, thank him for his cooperation and tell him how much you appreciate his effort. But if he says "No," pick him up, no dialogue involved, and carry him out. Even if he is crying and screaming and kicking, remain calm and carry him out to the car without saying anything. Drive away and don't feel the need to converse until he is quiet and settled down. Then you can tell him that he was rude to you, he did not respect your request and that next time you go to that particular place he will have to stay home.

The very next day tell him you are going to the same place and that today he will stay home with his dad or a sitter because he could not behave properly when it was time to leave, but that tomorrow he can try again.

Then the next day tell him you are going there again and you would like him to come along because you know he can cooperate.

If you go and he gets sassy, repeat the same process. Pick him up and leave. However, if he cooperates, thank him for listening and cooperating and remind him that you will be delighted to bring him with you next time.

The most important thing here is that you are consistent about the behavior you expect. You must follow through and do not give in to his lack of cooperation. Every time we give in, our children will try that trick 10 more times in hopes that it will work again. Every time we stick to our plan and do not let them call the shots, they will cooperate 10 times faster.

Chapter 28:
Toy Guns

Q: *So what about using toy guns? I really don't like them, I don't buy them and I don't want him to play "guns" or "weapons." My son is five and he turns his blocks into guns despite my protests.*

A: If the rule at your house is that children do not play "guns," then that's it. In teaching any rule, you need to be the enforcer, and you need to be the creative activity director.

Tell him that playing with guns is not allowed. They are dangerous and they hurt people. They are not a toy. Then offer suggestions about turning that block into a magic stick that makes things disappear or offer to help him build a huge castle with those blocks.

Remember that aside from teaching him what you do not want, you should help foster his interest in other activities. "Let's build a magic rocket ship and make space outfits out of construction paper and travel to cool planets and go exploring." Or, "Why don't we make a treasure map of the yard and I will hide a box with a secret treasure and then whoever finds it can have a turn hiding it and we will make another map."

> Q: *But I like to spend time with my son watching "Star Wars" because we both love it. I try to get him to use the light wands as something besides a weapon, but he always says, "No that's not what they do."*

A: Perhaps five is too young for him to be watching this movie if it is encouraging inappropriate behavior. There are a million activities to do that do not involve viewing violence. Find a movie that you can watch together that sets good examples, and watch "Star Wars" after he goes to bed.

Chapter 29
Lies about My Child

Q: *My son is in a Kindergarten class with a boy, Jerry, who makes up lies about my son to get him in trouble. Jerry's mom believes everything he says! I never talk to this woman, but I do run into her at school and she tells me things that her son has said about my son. My son gets off the bus crying saying that Jerry made up another lie about him. This time her son wrote a note to mine that said 'Stop hitting me.' My husband called Jerry's mom and asked if something happened that we should know about. She said, "No, Jerry said that was a class assignment, to write your feelings to someone in the class."*
My husband called the teacher – there never was such an assignment. I feel so sad for my son; I know he is not perfect, but generally he is a really kind and generous kid. What can I do?

A: One of the most difficult things to accept as a parent is that there is really nothing you can do about how other people parent.

This is such an unfortunate situation. (But remember that kids are much more resilient than we are as parents.) First, I would contact the school and be sure your son is placed in a different classroom next year away from Jerry. If you'd like, you could ask if they can move him now for the last few months of this year.

As for your son, tell him that he is a wonderful boy and that you want him to always be gentle to other people and to be honest.

These are situations that we can only make positive by learning from them. You can have conversations with your son about friendship and what that means and about what kind of person he would like to have as a friend and how he should treat other people. You can talk about honesty and how lies hurt other people. Tell him that sometimes you don't even know how much your choice of words can hurt other people. Explain that kids who lie, or are mean to other kids, are usually doing that because they want attention. Tell your son that you will always be there for him and you are willing to listen and talk about anything - that is what moms and dads are for.

Tell him how proud he should be for dealing with this situation. Remind him that he can walk away from this Jerry and choose not to listen to Jerry's lies. Reassure him that all kids are learning and that you hope that one day soon Jerry will learn to stop lying.

Because the boys are so young, I would intervene and alert the teacher. Tell the teacher what is happening so that your son does not get reprimanded at school for Jerry's tall tales about your son. If everyone is on board, maybe Jerry's lies will be ineffective and he will stop.

Chapter 30:
Fear of a Crowd

Q: *Bobby, age six, is experiencing fear at birthday parties. It's only birthday parties. It is weird and I am not sure what to do. He gets excited thinking about seeing his friends, he enjoys picking out the gift, but when he arrives at the party he gets scared. He covers his ears and doesn't want to stay.*

A: My guess is that he may be very sensitive to his environment. A previous party could have gotten out of hand and frightened him. For some children, being in a big group of friends where there is very little control and a great deal of chaos can be very overwhelming.

Being in school, in a group, or swimming class is different because there is so much supervision and monitoring. Birthday parties are often at a residence, with a large number of children and very few adults. The adults, although meaning well, may just not have the knowledge or skill to keep order with such a large number of active children. Some kids will thrive in that environment, some will go with the flow, and some will be overwhelmed and terrified by the out-of-control feeling.

It may have been one isolated action – a balloon could have popped right behind him, or someone may have pushed him, or it could just be a feeling of total chaos. Allow him his feelings, acknowledge them and offer to stay with him, or suggest that he get together with that child and just one or two others on a different day. He may not be ready to take on such loud, boisterous environments by himself. Try to restrict his social activities to a smaller, more structured group.

This is not a bad thing. Don't worry that he backs off from big, rowdy behavior. He just needs to mature and he will develop the confidence to handle those loud experiences in his own time.

Chapter 31: Time Out

Q: *When I put my son in his room for a time-out, he trashes the room. Now what do I do?*

A: Don't put him in there. You didn't say how long you leave him in there, but if he has time to trash the room, it's too long.

Leaving your son unattended in a fit of temper in his room only encourages him to create his own drama and to think of you as a tyrant. Long time-outs lead to more bad behavior and the original offense is long forgotten.

Try using a chair or the stairs. A time-out should never be longer than three minutes. Just long enough to say, "Your behavior is inappropriate, sit down for a minute, chill out, think about what happened and how you could have handled it differently, and go try again."

It helps to not even call it a time-out. If a behavior is disruptive, simply pick your child up, set him somewhere, not near anything fun, and say, "I asked you to stop that. You need to stand/sit here for a few minutes until you change your attitude and then come try again."

You want him to take responsibility and think, 'I have to be here until I can stop being crabby/hurtful/rude and then I can play again. So I need to take a breath and go try again because I want to play.' So then it is up to him to gain control of his emotions and be able to rejoin the activities.

Does that sound impossible? You'd be surprised! If you 1. remove him from the area every time his behavior is inappropriate, 2. give him a minute to calm down, 3. ask him to think of another way that he could have expressed himself, and 4. thank him for his effort and let him go try again, you will be amazed at how quickly he will take on that responsibility himself.

Seems an adult concept? I personally know three-year-olds who get it and say, "I am feeling angry and crabby so I am going to my room." Then they come back and announce to the world that they are feeling better and happy interaction starts right away which reinforces their decision.

We don't give kids enough credit for being able to be responsible for their own behavior. We think we need to micromanage. But in truth, if we involve children in problem solving, explain appropriate reactions or solutions, stay calm and follow through with consequences that make sense to them, then we will be absolutely amazed by the capabilities of our children.

Chapter 32: Reacts by Hitting

Q: *What do I do when my five-year-old daughter hits her playmate or her sister? Whatever the situation may be, her first reaction is to hit the other person.*

A: Remove her. When children inflict pain on another person, they must immediately see that it is an unacceptable way to treat another person and that, in so doing, she does not get to be near another person.

At the age of five, children can understand very mature conversations if they are presented with clarity and no temper. In a quiet moment when the two of you are together you need to have a conversation like this, "I have noticed when you are playing with a friend that you hit them when you get frustrated or angry. It is my job to not only keep you and your friend safe, but to teach you what to do when you feel angry. I will not allow you ever to hit another person and I will not allow another person to hit you. If you are frustrated with a friend, you have some choices. You can talk to her and tell her what is bothering you, you can just walk away from her and play alone or with another friend, or you can go into another room until you calm down and then come back in and play. If you need help remembering what to do, you can ask a grownup. If I see you hit again, I will pick you up, without conversation, and remove you from your friend for a while to help you remember it is never ok to hit. When you feel angry you need to walk away."

Now it is your job as a parent to be sure to closely chaperone your daughter. This is the hard part; we get caught up in laundry, dishes and paperwork. But even with all the chores we have, parenting has to come first. So if a situation arises, drop what you are doing immediately, and remove her. Pick her up and set her gently someplace safe, but away from any distractions and say in a low voice, "It is never ok to hit, you may not be near children if you hit them." Then take a deep breath, or walk away for a minute.

When the moment of anger has passed, go back to your daughter and ask her if she understands that hitting hurts and that it is never ok to do that. Tell her that you know that she can play gently and ask her if she feels ready to go try again.

It is crucial to always let your child know that you have faith in her abilities and that she gets to try again. This way she will develop self-esteem as well as self-discipline.

Note: Please be sure that you are role modeling appropriate responses when you feel angry. You can talk through what you are doing when you get mad to help her see that positive behavior in action. "I am very angry right now so I am going into the other room until I have calmed down and then we can talk."

Chapter 33: Picky Eaters

Q: *What can I do about my daughter not eating? The only way I can get her to eat anything is to give her dessert. So we have dessert after breakfast, lunch and dinner. She is five years old. Sometimes the only way I can possibly get her to cooperate with me is if I give her candy.*

A: Food for your child at this age is whatever you provide.

You may think that your child absolutely will not eat anything but sugar. But...the reality is that if it is not in the house, if there are no sweet things available, your daughter, at this age, will not starve herself to death. She may go hungry and be mad at you for not serving dessert. She may protest and refuse her next few meals. Let her. Stay calm, and tell her that breakfast is ready, and if she refuses to eat, do not make an issue of it. Just be sure there are no unhealthy snack foods available. If she gets hungry she can get an apple or a carrot, and eventually she will decide to join the family at the next meal.

Food should be presented as something that we eat in order to stay alive and healthy. If there are chips and soda and candy available, children will eat them, get full and reject dinner. If only healthy snacks are available then they will change their eating habits. They will actually acquire a taste for healthy foods. If you, the parent, cannot exist without chocolate, keep it at the office or on the top shelf of a cupboard, and eat it when the children are not home or asleep. Be a good role model in their presence. This is the only time in your child's life that you have the control over what they eat. If you wait until they are 10 to worry about their diet, they'll be over at friends' houses eating chips and candy. Take advantage of this time to expose them to healthy foods and build a good foundation for their diet.

Using food as a reward or punishment is not a good idea. When bribes involve food, such as: 'getting chocolate for going on the potty' or 'not getting candy because you hit your sister,' then food becomes a psychological and emotional manipulative tool. That can lead to much more complex problems.

Food should not be a prize, but a pleasant necessity to fuel our bodies. Teach your child that food is what gives her body energy, strength and health. And that is it.

Since your pattern of bribery is already established, you will need to talk to her about the existing routine and how that is going to change. Be very matter-of-fact and let her know that you are always learning how to be the best mom you can be for her. "I am learning new things all the time about being good at my job so sometimes I change my mind about something we have been doing."

Explain that you have learned more and now realize that three desserts a day is too much sugar for her body. So the new routine will be that you will be serving dessert once a day and she can have an apple before bed. Let her know also that when you ask for her cooperation, you expect her to try her best, but there will be no candy given out.

This doesn't mean she can never eat candy again. If your child understands that food is for staying alive and healthy, and it is not being used as a tool, then sometimes you can simply suggest, "Hey lets have a treat" for no reason at all. And that's the end of it. Don't make it a big deal. And if it hasn't been used for bribery, it won't be a big deal to the child.

****

Q: My son doesn't like what I make for dinner and wants me to make him something different. If I don't, he won't eat at all. What if he goes to bed without dinner? Is it ok for him to go to bed and not eat until morning?

A: Sure. In general, barring any medical needs, yes, it's ok to skip a meal or two. When he is hungry and knows that you are not going to cave in and bring out the snacks between meals, he'll decide to eat something offered. Your job is not to be a restaurant; you can't spend your life making three different dinners. When the family sits down to eat dinner together, he can eat what is there, or not. (Within reason. I wouldn't expect a child to eat snails or squid for dinner)

It has been said that one needs to see a new food on his plate 10 times before they try it. So keep trying. Don't assume that if he doesn't eat it once, he never will. Maybe serve one thing he likes and one new thing, but no sweets or chips in-between meals, and slowly his tastes will expand.

****

Q: *My son eats nothing. He has a fear of food because of his allergic reaction to dairy. We keep him alive on soy milk shakes and crackers, and that's all he eats. He has never had a scary reaction to anything; he was diagnosed with his intolerance for dairy as a baby. He refuses anything but crackers. There is a lot more he can eat and not react to, but he has gotten so freaked out about his allergies he will not try anything but crackers.*

A: Sometimes we talk out loud too much about what we are doing for our children. Stop all dialogue about food. If he has a fear of food, it is most likely a result of what he has heard around him. He needs to stop hearing people fret over him eating.

Be very matter of fact and tell him you will be serving foods that do not cause an allergic reaction and that he needs to eat more than crackers to stay healthy and strong.

Just put little portions of food he is not allergic to on his plate and get rid of all the crackers in the house and eventually, eventually he will start eating. Explain to him that, "Dad and I have been learning a lot about food and your body and we will not be providing crackers anymore but when you feel hungry you can try what we are eating. There are lots of great things you can eat that are dairy-free." Tell him you have spoken with doctors and learned that all the foods you will provide are safe for him and you love him and are doing the best you can to take good care of him.

****

Q: *Each morning I ask my children, "What do you want for breakfast?" but they all have different wants so most mornings I end up making pancakes, eggs, waffles, bacon and sausage!*

A: That's nice of you! Can you come live at my house?

Seriously, your job is not to be a short order cook.

I think it is nice to give children two choices. "You can have eggs or cereal."

****

Q: *My husband doesn't eat vegetables, and when I put them on the table he says to the children, "Yuck I wouldn't eat that if I were you." How will I ever get the children to eat greens?*

A: Something everyone needs to do with their spouse is discuss the things that are really important to you in child rearing. E.g.: "I can be willing to give on some things, but I feel that teaching our kids to eat a healthy diet is essential to their healthy future and I am asking you to support me on this. You don't have to eat anything you don't like, but please do not say anything negative about the food."

He could be a great role model in teaching the children to just try a new food. They don't have to eat it all, but after they try it a few times at various meals, they may decide they like it. So just keep offering healthy choices, to your children and your husband!

Working things out with your spouse is so important. It is crucial to hash things out in private and present things to the children as a united front. Otherwise they will always want dad to make lunch because he will never put a carrot in the bag.

****

Q: *My ten-year-old daughter wants to go off to camp, and I think it would be good for her, but I am afraid that she will not eat there. She swims every day and that is great but* *takes a lot of energy. Lately she eats little, if anything, and is getting rail thin.*

A: It's great that you are paying attention to this and not expecting the camp to do so.

You need to be straight with your daughter. Tell her it is a privilege to go to camp and a huge step to being independent. She has to earn that privilege by showing you that she is responsible enough to handle it. Tell her that her eating habits are worrying you. You understand that her swimming keeps her burning calories and you need to be sure she is eating enough to keep a balance. Let her know that you love her, want her to be safe and her body needs food to produce the energy and strength she uses in swimming. Explain that you would love to make camp possible if, in the next few months, she shows you that she is responsible about taking good care of her body and eating enough nutritious food.

Note: If she continues to eat next to nothing, and loses weight, trust your instincts and please consult your doctor.

Seven to ten years old

Every child
No matter their age
Needs an advocate
An adult who will stand up for them
Protect them
Love them unconditionally
Every child
Needs to know
That there is a person
Whom he can turn to
At any time
In any situation
Who will help him through the moment
With compassion
Without judgement
Every child
Deserves to be appreciated
For who he is
Because of his mistakes
Because he exists
Because
With one person who believes in him
He will keep trying
And have a future
Full of possibility

Chapter 34: Picking Up Toys

Q: *My eight-year-old refuses to pick up her toys. When asked to do so, she whines, screams and sulks. I yell, I get angry, and still I can never get her to help. It makes me so mad I want to throw all her toys away.*

A: Might not be a bad idea! By the age of eight, a child should absolutely be helpful around the house, particularly with her own messes.

First, I would limit the number of toys that are in her room. Dozens of toys in one place are too much for anyone to face. She can't play with them all at once, and pulling them all out just becomes something to do. So, put some of the toys in a few boxes and rotate which toys are in her room at one time. Start by having a small amount and tell her that when she shows you that she can manage to put them away when she finishes playing, that you will add a few more to the room. Explain that any toys left out will be removed because that will tell you that there are too many to manage.

Then follow through! It sounds like right now there are no consequences that are meaningful to her and perhaps you end up picking up alone so she sees no need to get involved?! Do not make threats you are not willing to carry out. Let her know that it is her responsibility to clean up her toys at the end of every day. She can do that throughout the day or wait until after dinner and go at it, but let her know that whatever is left out will be put away in the attic for a while until she can remember to pick up. Every day, calmly take the toys that are left out and put them away.

Don't get angry, just matter of fact. "I told you that the toys left out would be put away for a while until you can show me that you are able to pick up." If she gets down to one toy, then so be it. Remind her that if she picks up that toy then she can earn the right to have two more brought out. If she fusses and gets mad, just stay calm because ultimately you are giving her total control over whether she has her toys or not. She will have to make the decision to be responsible for her things. One day when she has a job, her boss is not going to watch her refuse to do her work and then pay her anyway. You are teaching her to be a responsible, reliable member of the family.

When she does pick up, thank her for being responsible and taking care of her things. Tell her that you see her making a real effort and you would like to bring back a few more toys if she thinks she is ready to take care of them. You have just avoided ineffective and potentially damaging yelling. Instead, you have presented her with a logical consequence which sets her on the road to self-discipline and rational thought. What a gift.

Chapter 35:
No Hitting – Ever!

Q: *When my twelve-year-old acts badly, my yelling has no effect on her. I want to hit her because I think she should know better, but I am not sure if hitting at this age is effective?*

A: Hitting at any age is not only ineffective but it is detrimental.

If we hit a child, she learns that...
1. It is ok for her to hit you or any person.
2. Adults are not to be trusted.
3. Sometimes people who love me, hit me. So perhaps if my boyfriend hits me up, it's ok because he loves me.

On the other hand, if we remove a child from the situation, tell her why the behavior was inappropriate, and ask her to go try again, she will learn that...
1. You have faith in her abilities.
2. She can believe in herself and start to check her own behavior.
3. Mistakes are part of learning.
4. If she keeps trying, she will succeed.

It is that simple..... and yet so very hard. We are creatures of emotion as well as intellect. And in stressful moments, our emotions often override our intellect.

So, how can we be sure we won't hit in a fit of anger? Walk away.

Whatever age your child is, if you are feeling frustrated and unable to think of a rational solution to the situation, explain that: "I am feeling so angry right now that I am not ready to talk about this yet. I need to be alone for a few minutes so I can talk calmly to you."

If someone else responsible is at home, take a short walk outside to clear your head.

Or, take a hot bath or just have a cup of tea and listen to calm music.

That old "count to ten" thing? Well, it really does take only about ten seconds for the anger to pass. Then give yourself another three minutes to relax and start thinking productively - without anger. Think of a way to handle the situation that will teach your child to be more respectful, responsible and cooperative.

If you need a helpful suggestion, call a friend, call a hot line, or pick up this book and read through a couple of chapters until you see an alternate way to handle what just happened.

And congratulate yourself for not hitting!

Remember, the way in which we discipline our children either makes them angry, confused and distrustful, or builds their self-discipline, confidence and trust in you.

Note: Setting firm limits is helpful to a child. Explaining the consequences of her behavior and allowing her to learn that there are limits helps her think about her actions and make wise choices. It builds her belief in herself as a capable human being and strengthens your communication and respect for one another.

On the other hand, hitting is demeaning and breaks down trust. She won't learn anything from what she did. Instead, she will lose respect and trust in you, and her own self-esteem will be negatively affected.

When you act out physically in anger, you abandon your sense of reason and logic and become ruled by power and rage. In terms of positive parenting to build self esteem, this is always detrimental.

Chapter 36:
Aggressive Behavior

Q: *My son is in second grade. He has a big temper and a demanding personality. We have worked very hard since he was two to help him learn to check his temper. Until now, he has been able to conduct himself well in school. But recently, the teacher has let me know that his behavior is at times rough and inappropriate. At home, I have noticed that while interacting with his father and me, he gets really mad and screams at us. I am so afraid I am failing him as a parent.*

A: First off, congratulate yourself on all the thought and energy you have used on behalf of your son. A child with a strong personality presents big challenges, emotionally and socially. You have obviously stayed on top of the game and helped him learn the skills with which to conduct himself in the school setting.

We cannot control how our children are genetically wired, but what we can do is help them understand their individual wiring and how to best deal with it in order to function successfully. Talk to your son about his outbursts, help him learn to notice when he is getting emotionally charged and give him a plan – to remove himself from the situation that is agitating him, and isolate himself until the feeling of anger has passed. Throughout his life he will run into people and situations that rub him the wrong way and learning how to cope successfully with those emotions is a gift you can give to him.

At home, if you are playing a game, and you notice that he is becoming emotionally charged, ask him if he'd like to take a break and start again later when he is calm. Try to help him see the situation before it bursts and realize that he can calm himself down and needn't push or scream.

Most importantly, keep communicating with him. Talk him through situations, explain the end result of aggressive behavior, role model calm behavior, and thank him for his self-control whenever he tries to use some.

Anger management is a major undertaking, but at his young age, starting to understand the concept of self-discipline is a huge bonus for him. Many people at 30 have not started understanding that concept yet! Helping him to notice when his temper is heightened, and to learn that he can walk away for a while or say nothing until he has calmed down and can use a polite voice, is a gift that will positively affect the rest of his life.

Chapter 37:
Sassy Mouth

Q: *What do I do about my ten-year-old daughter's sassy mouth? Whenever she talks to me it is with a snotty tone of voice or a demanding statement. I can't stand it, and when I tell her to stop, she rolls her eyes and says, "Whatever."*

A: First, always be an exemplary role model. <u>Always</u> use a polite tone of voice with her. You can be insistent and firm, but not rude when you speak to her.

Don't accept being spoken to rudely. Say to her, "I speak to you politely, I expect you to speak to me politely," or "Please think of a different way to say that to me that does not sound rude," or "Please go to your room and come back when you can talk to me politely." And do not engage in conversation with her until she has made an effort to change her tone. Remember that she hears these things at school and she needs to come home and try it. She may not know if it is an acceptable word or tone of voice, and the safe place to try it out is at home. Don't ignore it. She is hearing these things and needs to learn if they are appropriate to use or not. She is trying to sort through information she is getting outside of the house and needs a lot of guidance about what is and is not appropriate.

Explain to her that kids might say things at school, but that does not mean she can use those words, or attitude when speaking to you or anyone else. For instance, "whatever" may not seem a bad word, but with a snotty voice and shake of the head it is an incredibly impolite response. If you realize that she hears that tone from you sometimes, tell her that. Say, "You know I realize that I have used a rude tone of voice with you and that is where you learned it. Now I see that it is an inappropriate way to talk to someone and I am going to work very hard at changing my tone and I would like you to do the same." Children are very receptive to us admitting our flaws, recognizing the impact that we have and acknowledging that we care enough to want to change.

Chapter 38: Other Parent Blaming My Child

Q: *Whenever we get together with our good friends, their daughter, Sue, cries if my daughter, Lucy, doesn't spend every minute playing with her. Sue tells her mom that Lucy is being mean, when in fact Lucy has done nothing but choose to be alone for a bit, quietly reading a book or doing a puzzle by herself. Sue wants my daughter's undivided attention every second. Then Sue's mom comes to tell me about my daughter's bad behavior and how it is hurting Sue's feelings!! The girls are both age eight.*

A: The bottom line is that we cannot control how other people parent, much as we wish we could!

Sue's mom is doing Sue a huge disservice by coming to her rescue every time she whimpers, thus not letting Sue develop coping skills of her own. This would be a great opportunity for Sue's mom to teach her daughter about friendship and understanding.

But enough about Sue's family! Because again, we cannot control how other people act or parent.

What you can do is use the opportunity to teach your own child. Explain to your daughter that whenever we are socializing, there may be things that come up that bother us. But for the duration of time that we are with another person, we can choose to focus on those things that we enjoy about that friend, and try to ignore the behavior that is bothersome. Lucy does not have to play with Sue, nor does she need to run over and be Sue's caretaker. We certainly encourage our children to be compassionate towards others, but if this is an extreme situation of neediness, then we must also teach our children to stand up for themselves and that it is not wrong to politely turn down an invitation to play.

You can show Lucy that you are aware of and respect her feelings. The next time your families are getting together ask her if she would like to come along or would she rather play with a babysitter. We need to remember that just because we are friends as adults it does not necessarily follow that our children will want to be good friends and that is a choice they have the right to make.

Chapter 39: Teacher Picks on My Son

Q: *How do I talk to my son's first grade teacher and stop her negative treatment of him. Even other kids in the room say that she is hard on him. We have a sticker chart and he is losing stars at a great rate because we get yellow slips home from the teacher almost ever day; some are for his behavior, some are for something he forgot to bring to school.*
He doesn't even care about losing stars anymore. His grades are going down and he is more and more fidgety as the year goes on.

A: First, whenever you talk to another person, in this case a teacher, you should phrase things in a way that expresses your concern for your child, and not in an accusatory fashion. As parents, when our child is being treated wrongly, our protective lion instincts come out. However, if we use words that cause the person to whom we are speaking to get defensive, then they stop listening and communication is over.

When you talk to the teacher, phrase things in a constructive way, "What can we do together to help my son?" instead of in a negative way, "I really think what you are doing is wrong." Then try to state the facts as you see them, as pertaining to your son. "This is what I am observing: his grades are dropping and his attention span is shortening, his frustration is building and his interest in school is waning. What can we do as teachers and parents to get him back, ignite his interest and put him on a positive road?" Hopefully this will open some dialogue and start creative problem-solving while letting the teacher know you are actively involved in and concerned about your son's education.

You might mention to the teacher that you understand that some children can receive negative comments and let them roll off their backs, but there are others, like your son, despite his outward show of bravado, who take negative comments to heart. Ask her if she can help you think creatively about finding opportunities to say positive things that will help build your child's self-esteem and confidence so that he can behave appropriately.

When you talk to his teacher, put your thoughts into questions. Let her know that you are searching for the best answers for your son. You are his advocate and she gets to be with him more of his waking hours than you do. Since you both notice this negative downward slide, ask her what you and she can both do to turn it around. Tell her you are glad you can work together and to please keep in touch and give you the details of his behavior so you can better address them at home. It helps to know exactly what the situation was, instead of just a note saying he was loud. Ask, "Can you tell me specifically what he does to disrupt the room? Is this unusual energy or just an average boy's gross-motor behavior?"

The teacher will be more receptive to your concern if you state it in a positive fashion, "How can we excite my son about school? This is what I am noticing about him, and educating my son is the single most important thing I can do for him, so I want to find a way to help him love to learn."

Then at home, in a calm time and tone, you can ask your son about that specific situation and what he was feeling. Ask him how he dealt with the situation, and then brainstorm with him about how he could have handled it in a more appropriate fashion.

Q: *Doesn't it seem dumb to give a yellow slip for forgetting mittens or snow pants? That's my fault as his parent."*

A: I would let that go. All schools have certain rules that kids need to comply with. It is one step in learning to be responsible, so take that up with your child, not the school. Let him know that his job every day is to go to school, abide by the rules, and get himself educated. There will be rules in his future job as an adult that he doesn't like either, but if he wants the job, he will adhere to them. Suggest to him that you write a sign and put it on the front door saying 'Don't Forget!!' as a last minute reminder before he leaves for school.

Whether or not he likes his teacher this year, his job is to find something he can learn from her. Some years he will learn more than others, some years he will get along better with his teacher, but his job is to make life work for himself in this society and our job, as parents, is to help him develop the skills to do so. When you are in school that means not being disruptive and getting your work done. In the job market, it basically is the same!! These are life-long skills and you are doing him a great favor helping him figure it out in elementary school.

Q: *Aren't all boys filled with energy?*

A: Well, boys in general are wired for gross-motor activity right from the start. With that in mind, if your son has an abundance of energy that is coming out in the classroom, try getting a pile of pillows or a trampoline in the basement. Wake him up a little early so he has ten minutes to jump before going to school. Give him an appropriate place to release that energy.

At home, try to figure out what he is passionate about and tie that into his consequences. He needs to know that if his behavior at school is inappropriate, he cannot work with his model cars, or go fishing with his dad, or do something that is important to him. Then he will care enough to think about his behavior at home and at school.

Also, be sure to give him the opportunity to receive positive feedback. Thank him for even the slightest effort towards polite behavior. Kids need to see the positive results of their appropriate behavior. Sometimes we may only have a few opportunities to congratulate and thank them. If we miss those moments, they are only receiving the attention they get from their negative behavior, and they will soon decide that negative attention is better than no attention at all. So take the time to notice any small effort your child makes and make a big deal over it. Help him notice what he does that earns positive feedback.

Q: *Well, the other problem is that the other boys at school are behaving inappropriately. How do we help him to understand that just because someone else is doing it does not mean it is ok for him to do also?*

A: He can understand that. Explain quite simply that when other kids are doing something inappropriate, he can walk away. There is great power in walking away. It is a wonderful thing to teach your child, because ultimately you want him to have the strength of character to walk away from drugs and alcohol. If he is feeling crabby and notices that he is about to say mean things, he can walk away and say, "I'll be back when I am in a better mood." Or if the kids he is playing with start to spiral out of control, he can say, "I'll play with you guys later," and walk away. He may whine at the suggestion and say that then he won't have any friends. But remind him that they are not really friends if they only like you when you are naughty. In fact they will eventually respect you for making a wise choice.

Get to know the boys in his class and try to set up some get-togethers with kids whom you see have good manners and make good choices. Let him develop relationships that are healthy and then if the "boisterous gang" at school gets too rowdy, he can move away from them and know he has other friends to be with.

Tell him you believe in him; tell him you know that he knows what is acceptable. Tell him that he can actually be teaching other kids to make wise choices by role modeling that behavior. Congratulate him every time you see him make a good choice no matter how small. "Wow, thank you for giving that to your sister. That was awesome sharing." Or, "Hey, congratulations, you just made a great choice; you are really growing up and getting wise!"

You will be amazed at what a young age he can learn self-discipline. "If you feel crabby, walk away so you don't say or do anything that will be rude, and if you are with someone who gets rude, walk away, don't let people treat you rudely." These are concepts he really can embrace and put into action.

Chapter 40:
Playground crisis

Q: *My son's teacher tells me that he is very aggressive on the playground. He has always been a kid with a quick temper, and we have worked very hard on controlling that. When he is in the classroom his behavior is wonderful, he is helpful and polite to the other kids. He is so upset about this report and I don't know how to help him. My son is very sensitive and it upsets him that he is having trouble on the playground but he cannot tell me what happens or why. He is in second grade. What can I do?*

A: Playground activity is often one of the hardest times of the day for children. There is usually little adult supervision and kids can try out new behaviors knowing they are not being so closely monitored. Also, you mentioned that your son is sensitive which sadly may make him a target for any bullying behavior. Often kids like to pick on someone who is easily affected and shows a big reaction. Perhaps your son is in that category. I would suggest that you take a day off from work, if you need to do that, and go to his school at recess and observe. Tell him you are trying to find the best way to help him be successful and happy on the playground and you would like to come and watch for a day or two. Maybe being there you will notice behaviors or situations that trigger his aggression and then you can more specifically discuss it with him and help him know there are other ways to handle what is going on.

Whatever the triggers may be, the bottom line is that he needs help in learning to walk away. Talk him through several situations and show him that engaging in aggressive behavior can get him into trouble with the teacher, causes him to be labeled the bad kid on the playground and drives away other children's interest in being a friend.

Then explain to him that when he is in a situation that is causing his temper to rise, he needs to notice that he is getting worked up and then walk away from the situation. If in fact other kids are egging him on, if he walks away and shows no reaction, they will loose interest in bugging him.

For a child who is prone to quick anger or aggression, walking away is a necessary tool, one that will change his life. If he can start learning that technique now in second grade he will be a huge step ahead.

Keep up your good work, visit his school and try to help him identify the triggers, and remind him to always walk away and not get sucked in to children's taunting. They are not friends and he will be better off playing by himself than continuing to engage in activities with children who lead him to anger.

Chapter 41:
Fifth Grader Doesn't Care

Q: *My daughter is in fifth grade. She is as smart as a whip, very mature for her age and one of the oldest in her class. Recently, however, she has just started being very sloppy with her work saying that it is too easy and dumb. She forgets to bring assignments home, and just disregards reading projects. She also is being quite mouthy towards me, then I get upset and we end up yelling at each other and I am exhausted.*

A: Do not engage in verbal battle. This type of conflict is often very interesting for children with creative minds. They love to see the reactions and see if they can outwit the players. By engaging in verbal conflict, we are accepting that very behavior. Refuse to go there with her. Calmly remind her of the rules of the house and walk away. Give her no fuel for the fire then she will have no reason to carry on.

It is not unusual for very bright children to start to notice that they are bright and think that the assigned work is stupid. As parents, we need to help them find creative ways to make that work interesting for them. It is, after all, their job to get the best education they can, and our job to help them be successful in that job.

I would start by sitting down with her and telling her that you have decided there will be a few ground rules. During this chat be sure you are not in any way attacking her efforts or even commenting on her work; you are calm and non-emotional. Explain that since she is older, you will be giving her more responsibility to take care of her own work. School is her job and she needs to be mindful of her approach and effort. Your job as her parent is to help her build the skills to do her job successfully. Therefore, you will ask her for her homework each evening two hours before bedtime so that you can look it over. If it looks as if she put in effort, she has two hours of free time. If it seems slap- dashed together, she will be asked to redo it. That way the ball is in her court.

I would add that if her academics slide in a way that shows she is truly not making an effort, then the extra curricular activities will be pulled. Education is the most important key to her future and that must have priority.

Regarding the assignments that are not interesting to her, help her start to think out of the box. If the assignment is to read a chapter, ask her to read it and then do a painting of the main character. If the job is to do a math fact sheet, she can do it and then build a structure of toothpicks using the math principles she is learning. If the workbook is about life in the early West, use sugar cubes, glue and spray paint to build an old western town. Help her start to think beyond what is assigned, making it more exciting for herself, and soon she will be coming up with great ideas of her own.

Chapter 42: Bright but Pushing Obnoxious

Q: *My middle school daughter has a smart mouth. I can see that as a young girl, her father and I were so impressed with her quick wit that we may have encouraged this, but now it is becoming rude. I feel as if we messed up and am not sure how to approach it now.*

A: Being a parent is a hard job. Don't beat yourself up. Just be proud that you are noticing and wanting to make a change now on her behalf.

I would sit down and talk to her. She is obviously intelligent and of an age capable of having in-depth conversations. Perhaps something like this....

"There is no instruction manual for being parents. So every day and every year I am trying to be the best parent that I can. But I have to learn 'on the job' so to speak.

I realize that I have made some mistakes and I want to work on them. One thing I need to do as your parent is to help you learn how to communicate effectively with all kinds of people so that you can develop relationships, have jobs, and be a good friend.

You are very smart, and have a great sense of humor. However, I now see that because I have focused on that humor, I have done you a disservice because you are not able to see when using that sharp humor is or is not appropriate. So now I have to rethink my job to be a better guide for you.

I love you to pieces, and think you can do and be absolutely anything you put your mind to. And I want to help you develop the skills in communication that will open doors for you through the rest of your life.

So, here is the plan.

When I feel that you have said something at an inappropriate time, or in a rude way, I will stop you and say 'Please say that again and think about the words you are using.'

The thing is, that every person you talk to in your life will receive information from you in a different way. You need to learn to listen to people, be sensitive to them and see what type of words from you will make them feel comfortable. You may have one peer who uses smart remarks with you and you both think it is funny and are comfortable. But then you might be talking to someone else who is very sensitive and uncomfortable with sarcasm, and you need to adjust the way you are saying something. There may be kids at school who don't talk to you because they are put off by your smart answers and you don't even realize that you are offending them and they don't have a chance to get to know you.

Some people thrive on sarcasm and humor, and you may have many successful relationships with that form of communication. But one day, you might be talking to a boss who would be offended by a quick, sharp tongue. So I see that my job now is to help you recognize when your language is appropriate and when it needs to be modified. It is important to notice peoples' reaction to the words you use so you can carefully select the style of communication you use.

Language is very powerful. One sentence can make us laugh, cry, feel angry, hurt, betrayed or proud. So we need to really spend some time being aware of the effect our choice of words has on others.

I will help you by pointing out when I think you have chosen unwisely for the situation because I want to help you to be able to see it yourself and learn to self-correct. I will also make an effort to thank you when you use appropriate words and tone of voice.

I will try to be the best teacher I can be.

You are a fabulous young lady, and getting a handle on when it's ok to use a sarcastic line, or when to rethink the words you choose, will allow people to see what a gift you are."

Chapter 43:
How much truth to tell about sex?

Q: *At what age do you start talking about sex and how much do you tell a kid?*

A: You start the first time they ask a question, and answer it with total honesty. These questions come at very young ages.

It's pretty easy if you stick to answering just exactly what they asked. Don't give a lecture; don't elaborate. Usually they don't want lengthy details, just a simple direct answer to specifically what they asked. If they ask more, then answer more.

If you are as calm and matter of fact as you are when you answer their questions about gravity or the stars, they will feel safe in your honesty and happy to know they can come to you. Everybody has a body, all the girls have a vagina, all the boys have a penis, everyone poops... these are just facts, no big deal.

As they get older and the questions get more complex, be sure to keep talking, (even if you feel embarrassed because no one ever talked about these things with you). The more open you are the more likely they will come to you in times of serious decision making, and you will be so glad you opened those doors of communication. It is so much better that they get the correct information from you than some mis-information from a friend. You can also give them a book about our bodies; encourage them to understand their system, how it works, and why. Tell them you will be happy to answer any questions any time.

If you start conversations early, you will lay the groundwork for your child to feel comfortable talking about more sensitive topics as they enter middle and high school.

It is important to tell your teenage children that if they ever find themselves in an uncomfortable situation or they are scared, that you will talk to them about what has happened and will not make judgment. Remind them that you are there for information and help. In the moment of panic or crisis, it does no one any good to get emotionally charged and/or give lectures. Help them calmly to the best of your ability through the crisis, and find a later date to have a calm, but serious conversation about the choices they are making. Just don't harp at them when they are already in a panic or worried mode. Reassure them that you are there to help, to keep them safe, and to walk with them through the stormy days.

Eleven to seventeen years old

Please look at me
Allow me to grow
And to explore
And to find out for myself
Who I am
Do not try to mold me
Do not make me into something you want to show off
Instead, show off the fact
That you love me for exactly who I am
And for the choices I make
I am a capable human being with something to offer
Please look at me
And smile

Chapter 44:
Exposure to Different Rules

Q: *Is it wrong to discourage relationships with children from families that have different rules than ours? My eleven-year-old daughter has a friend who is very nice but her parents let her get away with murder and I don't want that to rub off on my daughter.*

A: Any time you discourage a relationship, that friend suddenly becomes all the more interesting!

What you have to decide is, is your child ready to go to a house alone where the rules may differ greatly from yours? For example, if your child can understand that she cannot drive the 4-wheeler even if she is at a house where it is permissible, let her go play there.

There will definitely be some houses that you won't want your children to go to. So let your children know that those children are welcome at your house. You are not trying to pick their friends, just being sure they are safe where they play. Be very blunt. Kids understand and appreciate honesty. Say it simply: "I am not comfortable with the rules at her house, but I'd be happy to have your friend come over here."

Keep repeating your rules. Sometimes you will feel exhausted by repeating yourself, but that is our job as parents. You wouldn't stop saying, "Don't touch the hot stove" to a one-year-old. You say it and say it until they finally get it. As teens, your repeated warning may be "Don't drive drunk." When they hear it for the fiftieth time and say, "Mom we know!" You can reply, "That's good, but I'm a mom and my job is to say it again."

Whatever the rules are, if they promote wise choices, safety and self-respect, they are worth repeating! And if your rules are clear and consistent, your children will take them with them wherever they go.

Chapter 45:
Friendship Trouble

Q: *My middle school daughter has been hurt by her best friend who lied to her and she is now slipping in her school work and having a bad attitude towards us. Usually she is an A student and very fun to be around. She has a good sense of herself and how to behave with other people. She doesn't think her friend is really sorry and she wants to talk about it but the friend says it is history. Her friend's behavior has really thrown her for a loop. How do I help her set this straight?*

A: The thing about any relationship is that each of us as individuals has to find where we draw the line. Any relationship has its moments. If a friend beats us up, we decide that she is not a friend and quickly end that relationship. If a friend says something sassy and then apologizes and feels remorse for saying it, then we can be forgiving of human error, accept the apology and resume the friendship. But then there is a lot of grey area between those two situations. What if the friend steals from you? What if the friend hangs up on you? What if the friend doesn't offer to pay her half of the bill?

What if she makes a face?

Any time we engage in a relationship with another person, there will be choices to make all along the way. There are questions we have to ask ourselves when we have mixed feelings about a friendship. Am I getting anything from this friendship? Am I being drained by this person? Am I being stubborn? Does this friend notice how hard I try?

So, what your daughter is going through right now is actually a great opportunity for you to help her learn about herself and what she will or will not tolerate from a friend and what friendship means to her.

What you cannot do, nor can your daughter, is change the way the friend behaves. Your daughter can choose to talk to the friend and tell her that she feels bad about how this is being handled. But in the end, she can only control how she herself decides to react to the chosen behavior of the friend. She can let it go and accept the apology, she can choose to end the friendship, she can tell the friend the situation continues to bother her and she needs to talk about it, or she can write her friend a letter explaining her feelings, among other things.

What can you do? You can let her vent. Acknowledge her feelings. Be a listening ear and respect what she chooses to do. You can also explain to her that you understand she has heightened emotions right now, and you respect that, but after thinking or talking about it for a while she needs to get back to her work and through it all she still needs to treat you with the same respect you offer her.

When we get emotional, we may need to stew a bit in the emotion and not deny it, but we also cannot allow it to engulf us and cause us to give up all the rest of the goings on in our lives. If we let a negative emotional situation completely take over our thoughts, we stop functioning. So you can explain to your daughter that she of course can feel hurt and angry and she should express those feelings by talking and writing and perhaps even sulking. Then she needs to find a place she can put those emotions, to refer back to when needed, so she can carry on and function successfully in her daily life.

This will ultimately be an education that will benefit her for the rest of her life in every relationship whether it is with a friend or a boss or a spouse.

Chapter 46: Quick to Give Up.

Q: *My child, age twelve, is very hard on himself. When he sees a challenge, he immediately says it is too hard. When he makes a mistake, he cries and says he can't do it. It makes me mad and sad for him, but I don't know what to say.*

A: Every opportunity you get, when he makes a small error, tell him that making mistakes is how we learn. If we never tried hard things and made mistakes we could never learn, so making mistakes is not a bad thing.

Also tell him that you have decided that the word 'can't' is no longer allowed in the house. He can say, 'Boy this is going to be hard,' or 'Do you think you could help me get started,' or 'Hmm, I think this will take me a long time.' By teaching him to phrase things in a way that instills hope and confidence and willingness to try, his attitude will change. It is remarkable what a powerful impact the words we use have on our mental state. If we phrase things in the negative, we actually start believing that we can't! If we look at things as a challenge, acknowledge their difficulty and tackle them anyway, we will start to believe we can do anything. That is what you want your child to learn by removing 'can't' from his vocabulary.

Find moments during the day, to recognize even the tiniest of things and say, "Wow! You tried and you did it!" or "Boy that looked hard to me and you were able to do it." He probably doesn't realize all the things he takes on and completes successfully because he has taught himself to focus on what he feels he can't do. Your little comments of admiration will make him start to notice all the small challenges he takes on and accomplishes. This will build his belief in himself.

Chapter 47: Daughter Wants to Quit Band

Q: *My thirteen-year-old-daughter wants to quit band and I don't know what to do because we think she should keep it up, but she went off to practice today crying. Now I am not sure we should be forcing her to stick with it.*

A: At thirteen you have to carefully choose your battles. Sex, drugs and alcohol have to be first. You need to keep the doors of communication wide open to help fight against these influences. Peer pressure is strong and your kids need to know that you will listen to them and be willing to compromise as you expect them to do with you. Have you talked to her about why she hates band?

Q: *No. She just has been saying she hates it for the past month or so and I just keep ignoring it and telling her she is going.*

A: Sit down with her. Ask her to break it down for you so you can better understand what she is feeling. What is it she hates: the music, the teacher, the uniform, the practice time? She may surprise herself when she does this and realizes that all her negative feelings are just about the uniform, and maybe it is silly to give up an instrument you love playing over an outfit. Or, you may be surprised to find that she really is not enjoying any of it any longer.

Then explain to her why you feel it is so important to you that she continue. "It builds your musical background; you'll be glad as an adult that you can play an instrument; music awakens parts of our brain we may not use otherwise; it is a fabulous education in discipline and self-motivation; it is great to be a part of a group of music lovers who work toward a common goal." This will help her understand your point of view and may have an impact on the final decision between the two of you.

Let her know that you are considering what she has said and that perhaps in light of the conversation you feel that she should try to stick it out for another year, or that you have decided that this is something you can be flexible about and she can drop it.

Remember that there are so many subjects in and out of school that you cannot be flexible about regardless of her feelings, i.e. Math, English, Biology, all the classes she has to take and the fact that she needs to work as hard as she can to bring in decent grades so that doors are open for her future. These academic pursuits are non-negotiable to many families. Drugs and alcohol are non-negotiable to many families. So, when it comes to extra-curricular choices, you need to make a huge effort to have open discussions. We need to really listen and find some things that we can say "Ok, I see your point of view and even though I don't agree I am willing to respect your feelings," and go with it.

And realistically, if she truly dislikes band and is crying before she goes, she probably is not reaping all the great benefits from it that you had hoped. So, you may want to use this as one way of showing her how open and understanding you can be and that you respect her feelings and are a trustworthy advisor.

Chapter 48: Apathetic Teen

Q: *My fifteen-year-old son spends 70 percent of his time in his room. He says he is reading. If he were, I might not be concerned because at least he'd be learning. He says he is talking to friends, but as far as I know he has only one friend, the only friend who has ever come over to our house or to whose house our son has been. I ask him if he wants to play basketball or cards, he says, "No thanks, I'll be in my room." His grades are fair to poor and he does not like school nor does he want to go to college. Should I be worried or is this typical teenage behavior?*

A: It is true that teens do like the privacy of their room to chat with friends, listen to their music, and write notes. Not wanting to engage in activities with you seems very normal.

No one knows your son as well as you, and if your instincts are telling you that something is just not right, you should listen. His general lack of enthusiasm for school and his future along with a seemingly small peer group deserves attention. Is this due to depression, fear of failure, lack of self-confidence, sense of abandonment? Does he seem content on his own, cooperative and functional when asked to participate?

Be proud that you are noticing and want to be of help. At fifteen, if you do not have open communication with your son, it will not begin overnight. Don't expect him to sit up with you all night and reveal his inner-most feelings. Instead, talk to your son and tell him that his lack of interest in anything, and his fairly anti-social behavior are causing you concern and, as his mom, your job is to try to keep him safe and happy. Tell him you understand that kids often do not like to talk to their parents at this age. If he would rather not talk to you, then you would like to help him find a counselor, an uncle, or a teacher with whom he would feel comfortable talking.

Meanwhile, set some limits in the house. Respect his privacy but also require some family participation. He can stay in his room for a max of three hours. After that you will come get him and ask for help with some project that needs doing in the house such as painting, cleaning, or laundry. It is important to expect some interaction as well as some involvement in the running of the house in which he lives. Keep talking, check in with his school and ask the teachers how he seems during the day. Find an interest of his and a way for him to put it to use. He could help coach little league or volunteer in an art studio. Explain that you are concerned and need to see him actively participating in his life just for a few hours a week. Keep talking and listening closely and seek help if you feel the need.

Chapter 49: Sleeping late

Q: *My daughter is sixteen and she has zero interests.*
She sleeps until 2 or 3 P.M. every weekend, and spends all her time in her room on the phone. She does nothing in the house, has no hobbies, doesn't like to read, hates school, and rarely talks to us. She only likes to hang out with her friends. What can I do?

A: Sleeping late is a favorite pastime of teenagers, but I would put a cap on it. Tell your daughter she can sleep until 10 or 11 A.M., and then tell her she will be getting up to join the family for lunch and conversation. Sleeping until 2 or 3 P.M. every weekend seems to be a great avoidance technique – avoiding life in general.

You may chat with her school counselor about getting her involved in some volunteer program after school or on weekends. Find two or three age appropriate activities/programs and tell her she gets to pick one. She then has some choice in the matter but she must participate in one or the other.

By letting your daughter continue to do nothing, in a silent way, you are telling her that is ok. Instead, put limits on the unproductive time and find interesting groups in which she can participate. Then she can start to see that perhaps she enjoys doing something, or at least that she can feel successful and helpful at whatever it is she is doing.

Chapter 50:
Her Friend is So Mean

Q: *My teenage daughter has a friend who is so mean to her. She torments her, makes fun of her, leaves her out - this has gone on for years. The friend's mother is a friend of mine. I think I want to talk to my friend about her daughter's behavior.*

A: Don't. This is between the two girls. It is for your daughter to sort out and decide what she wants to do.

If you talk to the mom, you may make her defensive and resentful and that will add yet another layer of discomfort for your daughter. Your friendship with the mom is totally separate from the girls' relationship.

Our job as parents is not to rescue our children, not to curtail other kids' behavior, but to give our own child the coping skills with which to deal with all the people they will encounter in their lives. Our job is to help them learn to sort through what they will or will not accept, where they draw the line and when they choose to walk away.

We all have to find out where we draw the line. We may put up with some negative behavior from a friend because the rewards of the friendship far outweigh those moments. We may put up with a negative tone of voice from a boss because the pay check is huge. But when do we stop? When do we decide that the positives are not worth putting up with the negatives? That is an individual call. What you can do for your daughter now is to have conversations about what friendship means and what behavior she is willing to accept from her friends.

Does your daughter think this girl really is a friend if she is continually rude to your daughter? Is that the way your daughter wants to be treated by a friend? Or should she back off from that friendship and make new ones. We need to let our children know that it is ok to move on. Explain to her that: "As you grow and mature you discover what is important to you and what values you hold dear. In so doing you may well choose new relationships, and new friends, and that is fine. It is the process of growing up. You may decide to stop dating your boyfriend, or to hang out with a new group of girls, or to just spend some time on your own".

As parents, we get so accustomed to intervening. And when our children are young this is indeed our job. If your daughter were four, I'd say, yes, talk to the mom, or better yet, don't take her to that house to play anymore. We have so much control when they are young. But as the parent of a teen, our job is not to do for them, but to teach them the skills they need to cope with whatever comes their way. Teach them that they are completely capable and that they need to respect themselves and walk away from anyone who does not treat them with respect.

So don't talk to your friend about your daughter. Instead, talk to your daughter – about values, friendship, tolerance and abuse.

Then let your daughter talk to her friend, or not. Let her decide what she wants to do about the situation.

PARENT HANDBOOK

Chapter 51: Curfew

Q: *My sixteen-year-old daughter is angry with us for setting a curfew of 11:00 p.m. We don't think this is unreasonable, but she says all her friends can stay out later and if we are so strict about a curfew she will just have to sneak out. She is really a good kid. Her grades are good, she cooperates with us, helps around the house and I wonder if we are being too strict. My husband is dead set on this curfew.*

A: When our children get to be young adults, we must relinquish more and more of our ultimatums allowing them to eventually be in charge of themselves. That is a difficult transition for us. They are becoming adults and we need to notice the times that a compromise will do more for building trust and respect than sticking to our inflexible rules. When our kids are two and three, we just tell them what to do because we are the adults and they don't have the knowledge to make wise choices on their own. By sixteen if they are kind, reliable, and generally cooperative, be thrilled, and make allowances and start letting out the tether and letting them make some more difficult choices. That is how we help them prepare to live on their own.

So, first, the mere fact that she is telling you that she finds the rule too severe and that she may have to sneak out means that you have darn good communication with her and she is being very honest. Thank her for her candor and tell her you are willing to listen and work on this with her.

If we are totally inflexible with no room for conversation and negotiation, then we teach our children to lie and sneak around and not communicate with us. This is a good way to get her to start doing things wrong after all the effort she has made to make wise decisions.

I would tell her that you will take each event on a case by case basis. One night if you are comfortable with who she wants to go out with and where she is going, tell her to come home when she thinks it wise - but also ask her to give you a call after 12:30 so you know she is safe and at that time she can tell you when she will be home.

If she were going someplace you are not terribly comfortable with, you could just remind her of the potential life-altering consequences that bad choices make, ask her to call you at 11 P.M., check in, and go from there—you could let her stay if she said things were fine and she was being smart.

If the plans were such that you could not be comfortable letting her go, just tell her, "We work with you each night you go out and often you make a good case to go and not have a specific curfew. Now we are telling you that we are not comfortable with this situation and we need you to work with us. Let's brainstorm together about alternative plans."

If you involve her in the problem-solving then you'll come up with a solution you both can live with and teach her a great skill in the process.

The bottom line is, you have laid the ground work, she is a good kid, now you have to let go and believe in her. She will make the right choices if she sees that you believe she will.

Always require that she wake you up when she gets home. Don't ask many questions. Just "Did you have fun? Great. Thanks for making good choices. Good night." Then you know she is home safe, she sees that you have respected her maturity and ability to make smart decisions and you can tell if she is in an altered state. Be totally honest about that and tell her that by chatting with her upon her return and seeing what condition she is in, you can feel confident about the choices she is making. If she slips into the house and races to her room, you should be totally uncomfortable with what is not being said.

Make it clear that you will trust her ability to make wise choices and be honest with you. Should she decide to break that trust, the boom will fall hard, the car will be gone, and a stiff curfew will resume because she will have shown you that indeed she is not yet ready to make her own smart decisions and still needs you to set the rules for her.

Keep talking to your daughter and keep trusting her because you need those lines of communication open so when she does get scared or uncertain she will call you!

Chapter 52: Dad's Difficulty with Dating Daughter

Q: *My teenage daughter wants to go to her boyfriend's house and my husband thinks that is inappropriate even though this boy's parents are home. He also will not let them be in her room, even with the door open. She does not want to sit in the living room because our house is very open and we can hear everything. What should I do? She is sixteen and she is a great kid with straight A's in school and wonderful social manners.*

A: Tell your husband to think carefully about his two choices here. One is to communicate and compromise with his daughter so she feels respected and trusted, another is to close that door of cooperative negotiations and she will start lying.

These are serious years. Life is not as safe as it was when your husband grew up. Our kids have to be able to talk to us and run things by us for honest and reasonable ideas.

We have to bite our tongues and be flexible and yes, talk to them. We now need to allow them to make decisions and have faith in all the hard work we have put into them thus far.

We have to trust them to be good decision-makers. Tell your daughter that you will trust in her ability to think clearly and make good choices. If someday she breaks that trust, then the consequence will be severe, (i.e. the car will go, the dates will be chaperoned) but that you don't expect that to occur, and you are proud of her and her wise choices.

Talk to her openly about the serious results of her choices at this age. Ask her what she might think her life would be like if she were pregnant or had AIDS? Have these conversations without anger or judgment, just to open her eyes to the realities of life as a young adult.

Leave the door to communication wide open. She needs to know she can say anything to you and you will be a helpful advisor, not a judgmental parent; that you will help her work through the difficult and confusing times in her teen years, and that you will be there for her. Otherwise she will shut you out and go to her peers and, believe me, her peers do not always give useful advice!

After all the years you have spent helping her thus far, why would you close her out and miss out on the most fantastic part of the relationship? If you unreasonably instill rules and limits that are unjustified, she will turn away and possibly not return. These are the years when you become trusting adults. If you keep the communication open and positive, she will remain close the rest of your life.

Chapter 53:
Parent Attacks My Parenting

Q: *My daughter has a friend who is very tricky and often hurts my daughter's feelings. This has gone on for years and the girls are now seventeen.*

Recently, the friend's mother has emailed me to complain about some of my daughter's behavior as reported by her daughter! The girls are not getting along and she wants to know what the problem is and is basically blaming my daughter for everything that has transpired between the two and attacking my parenting. I don't know this woman very well and I don't think she has any right to attack me and my daughter's behavior. She says I should open my eyes and make my daughter apologize. Apparently she is telling everyone she sees about my shortcomings as a parent!

I am livid. I don't want my daughter to be labeled and gossiped about. And this mother is saying things that just are not true. I want

> *to write back to her, but am not sure what to say without sounding really angry.*

A: Don't write.

If she were your partner or your best friend in the whole world and you couldn't live without her, I'd say, lock yourselves in a room and hash out all the details that are causing grief to save the partnership. (Even under those circumstances, talk face to face, don't write. Printed words have no inflection, no facial gestures, and can be easily misconstrued. When you have an important emotional conversation that needs to take place, have it in person so you can watch each other's reaction and clear up any misunderstanding immediately.)

In this case, I'd stay away. People who write or call and attack you and your children, are just opening the door for you to come unhinged, to say a lot of things that you didn't mean to say, to get defensive, and then they will turn around and gossip about all you said with new ammunition.

If she pursues it, tell her that your daughter and her daughter have a friendship and they are seventeen years old and it is their job to handle their friendship as they choose and that you will not be involved in it.

That is part of being a parent of a teen - letting your children handle their own affairs. We can give them solid advice and suggestions if we are asked, but ultimately they have to sort through and decide if that friendship is truly a friendship or an unrewarding struggle.

Often parents like this want to rescue their children. They intervene any time anything goes wrong in their child's life. And sadly, they do not realize that they are robbing their child of the opportunity to cope and see that they are indeed capable, competent young adults.

If you feel you absolutely must write back, make it very simple, nothing she can come back at you with. Something like this:

Dear X,
Parenting is such a hard job, and we all do the very best we can do.

I have faith that at seventeen, our daughters have the skills to work out their own difficulties.

Sincerely, Y

Chapter 54: Letting Teens Drink

Q: *My son wants to have a party at our home and wants us to let his friends drink. They are all seventeen and eighteen. He says other parents let this happen because they'd rather have the kids at home drinking than out on the streets.*

A: Drinking underage is illegal. End of story.

I do not have my head in the sand. I know kids drink under age. If you choose to let your own teenagers have a drink in your own house that is totally up to you.

However, to have a party at your house and serve drinks is breaking the law. You are taking the lives of other people's children into your care. As a parent, at a party, your job is to adhere to the law and be a role model.

If a minor had been drinking at your house and had driven home and had a wreck, you would be liable. If a minor were drinking at your home and you didn't know he had taken drugs beforehand, and he had a heart attack due to the combination of poisons in his system, and he died, you could be held responsible.

Explain this to your son, and suggest that you will put up a volleyball net, a dart board and/or pool table for entertainment. Put the speakers outside and have great music and lots of pizzas.

As much as your son will whine and may never have a party at your house, your steadfast example and interest in safety and wise choices will have a huge impact on him.

Conclusion

Parenting is the single most important job you will ever have.

The two absolute necessities from us as parents are Consistency and Respect. Consistency and Respect. With consistency, children develop self-confidence, trust and esteem. Without it they are confused and scared, and develop fear, distrust and self-doubt.

Respect builds trust, cooperation and compassion. Being treated with a lack of respect causes children to stop communicating with us, stop listening to us, and stop trusting in us. Treating others with respect opens doors to an enjoyable, successful relationship and the great bonus is that we are treated that way in return.

To achieve consistency and respect in our relationship with our children, there are three key ingredients:

Love, Communication and Guidance.

Love. Children need to know that they are loved unconditionally, not contingent on their behavior or successes, but purely because they exist. Feeling loved is essential to children's development. Yet a family brimming with love, but without guidance or clear communication, leads children to a state of chaos and frustration.

Communication. The words that we choose to use when speaking to our children can help them build-self esteem, encourage problem-solving, and foster independence. Words can also demean, intimidate and reject. The specific choice of words we use and how we deliver a message play an important role in the images your children develop of themselves, as well as in the quality of the relationship between you and your children.

Guidance. You are the role model, the teacher. The way you conduct yourself has a greater impact on your children than even the words you say to them. You set the standard and the example for acceptable behavior. The choices of consequences you use, and how you implement those consequences, will help to either develop or deteriorate the trust and respect between you and your children.

With a balance of these three ingredients, you and your children will travel through life enjoying the journey. You will come out strong, with children who believe in themselves and trust in your love for them.

Today is the day for you to be building and developing a great relationship with your children through effective communication, respect and understanding. Being a parent means that you have to make some unpopular decisions that may not be to your children's liking. But if you are using positive communication skills, and treating your children with respect and understanding, your parenting will be effective and appreciated in the end. The hours you put in now will pay off many times over for the rest of your lives.

If you have a question you would like to see in "The Parent Handbook - Volume II", please e-mail it to: leslie@theparenthandbook.org

Made in the USA
Charleston, SC
08 December 2012